CORSETS and CRINOLINES

1 *c.* **1460.** A Spanish mediaeval painting showing the ladies wearing stiff bodices and artificially-shaped skirts: the beginning of the "boned body" and the "farthingale"

Colección Muntadas, Barcelona

CORSETS AND CRINOLINES

By

Norah Waugh

Theatre Arts Books

Second Printing, 1970

Copyright 1954 by Norah Waugh

Library of Congress Catalog Card Number: 69-11134

Published by

Theatre Arts Books
333 Sixth Avenue
New York, N. Y. 10014

Manufactured in the United States of America

CONTENTS

ACKNOWLEDGMENT

FOR permission to examine specimens of garments, and for technical information supplied, the Author would like to thank the Victoria and Albert Museum, the London Museum, the Gallery of English Costume, Manchester, the Österreichisches Museum für Angewandte Kunst, Vienna, Mrs. Doris Langley Moore, and Messrs. R. and W. H. Symington and Co. Ltd., Market Harborough; also the Bayerisches National-museum for kindly sending her the pattern and description of their rare early whaleboned bodice. She is also grateful to Mrs. Kay West for her assistance and advice in compiling the Index and Glossary, and to the many friends who have helped her in her search for material.

The Author and the Publishers are indebted to the following for their kind permission to reproduce the illustrations in this book:

Messrs. Berlei (U.K.) Ltd., for fig. 49; the Trustees of the British Museum, for fig. 31; Messrs. Charles Bayer and Co. Ltd., for fig. 82; Colección Muntadas, Barcelona, for fig. 1; Messrs. Dickins and Jones Ltd., for figs, 65, 66, and 70; the Director of the City Art Gallery, Manchester, for figs. 91, 95, and 96; Messrs. Harvey Nichols and Co. Ltd., for fig. 84; Messrs. J. S. Blair and Son Ltd., for figs. 74 and 83; The London Corset Co. Ltd., for fig. 71; the Trustees of the London Museum, for figs. 10 and 21; The Royal Worcester Warehouse Co., for fig. 67; Messrs. Spiers and Pond Ltd., for fig. 68; the Director of the Victoria and Albert Museum, for figs. 5 and 11; the Director of the Wallace Collection, for fig. 4; Messrs. A. M. Wicks, for fig. 81; the Dean and Chapter of Westminster Abbey, for figs. 22, 23, and 24.

They are also grateful to Mrs. Gwen Raverat for her permission to quote from *Period Piece*, published by Messrs. Faber and Faber Ltd., and to Messrs. Martin Secker and Warburg Ltd. for their permission to quote from Colette's *Mes Apprentissages*.

LIST OF ILLUSTRATIONS

BIBLIOGRAPHY

CIBA Review No. 46, *Crinoline and Bustle*, 1943.

Corset and Crinoline, 1867.

Diderot and d'Alembert, *Encyclopédie*, t. IX, 1751.

Fizelière, Albert de la, *Crinoline au temps passé*, 1858.

Kelly, F. M., *Farthingales*, Burlington Magazine, Vol. XXI, 1916.

Leloir, Maurice, *Paniers et Crinolines*, Bul. I., Société de l'Histoire du Costume, 1913.

Léoty, Ernest, *Le Corset à travers les âges*, 1893.

Libron, F. and Clouzet, H., *Le Corset dans l'Art*, 1933.

———

Boehn, Max von, *Modes and Manners*, 1927.

Challamel, Augustin, *The History of Fashion*, 1882.

Cunnington, C. W., *The History of Underclothes*, 1951.

——, *Englishwomen's Clothing in the Nineteenth Century*, 1938.

——, *Englishwomen's Clothing in the Present Century*, 1952.

Davenport, M., *The Book of Costume*, 1948.

Fairholt, F. W., *Costume in England*, 1896.

——, *Satirical Songs and Poems on Costume*, Percy Society, 1849.

Kelly, F. M., and Schwabe, R., *Historic Costume*, 1925.

Laver, James, *Taste and Fashion*, 1937.

Leloir, Maurice, *Histoire du Costume*, VIII, IX, X, XI, XII, 1933.

——, *Dictionnaire du Costume*, 1951.

Linthicum, M. C , *Costume in the Drama of Shakespeare*, 1936.

Planché, J. R., *History of British Costume*, 1874.

Quicherat, J., *Histoire du Costume en France*, 1877.

Also Contemporary Magazines, Journals and Memoirs.

BIBLIOGRAPHY
MUSEUM AND PRIVATE COLLECTIONS

Victoria and Albert Museum, London. Seventeenth- and eighteenth-century boned bodices and corsets, crinolines, and bustles—rare early specimens.

London Museum, London. Seventeenth- and eighteenth-century boned bodices and corsets, paniers, crinolines, and bustles—rare early specimens.

Gallery of English Costume, Manchester. Corsets from the middle of the eighteenth century, crinolines, and bustles—a large and varied collection, especially of the latter.

Mrs. Doris Langley Moore, London. Private. Corsets from the middle of the eighteenth century, crinolines, and bustles—an interesting and representative collection.

R. and W. H. Symington and Co. Ltd. Market Harborough. Private. Corsets, metal corset moulds, and corset embroidery samplers—a unique collection of the corsets manufactured by this firm from 1854 to the present day.

CHAPTER I

Beginning of the Sixteenth Century to 1670

1

THE WHALEBONED BODY

THE soft, flowing lines of the mediaeval period followed the natural figure; no artificial shape was given to the body. Of course it is quite likely that about the middle of the fourteenth century, when clothes began to mould the figure, the older woman who had lost her shape, or the woman who had never had one, wore her under-robe of stouter material and laced it more tightly; and when in the fifteenth century the waist became high and small an extra band of stiff material may have helped to make her "middle small"; but it is unlikely that any artificial stiffening was added. Such an undergarment was called a "cotte", an early French word for any close-fitting garment (Fr. *côte*—rib)—various names for dress are derived from it, e.g. petticoat, waistcoat, etc. The word "corset" when found in mediaeval texts applies to an outer garment and was not used in the modern sense.

By the middle of the fifteenth century the long, spiring mediaeval lines had been stretched out to their utmost limit, e.g. by means of hennins, peaked shoes, etc., until finally a reaction set in and towards the end of the century both men's and women's clothes began to assume a new, broad, straight silhouette. This silhouette was very much influenced by the Renaissance style which was slowly spreading northwards. The great development of the silk industry in Italy and Spain had made rich silks, brocades, damasks, velvets, etc., the fashionable materials, and their stiffness, weight, and elaborate patterns required a more severe treatment than that used for the softer woollen materials more commonly worn earlier. The new style of dress came from the south, so it is not surprising that Italy is usually credited with the invention of the "busc", the first artificial support to the body, and Spain the "farthingale", the first artificial aid to the skirt. It is said that Catherine of Aragon brought these fashions to England, while the Italian wars of the French kings Charles IX and Louis XII brought them to France; they would probably have come anyway.

When in England and France at the beginning of the sixteenth century the separation of the bodice and skirt became fashionable, it was possible to make the bodice straighter and tighter and the skirt fuller. In order to keep the bodice straight and tight a heavy under-bodice was now worn, and in this the women were imitating the men, who from mediaeval times had worn such a garment under their outer ones; it had been known by various names—cotte, gambeson, doublet, pourpoint, etc.—and in the sixteenth century

17

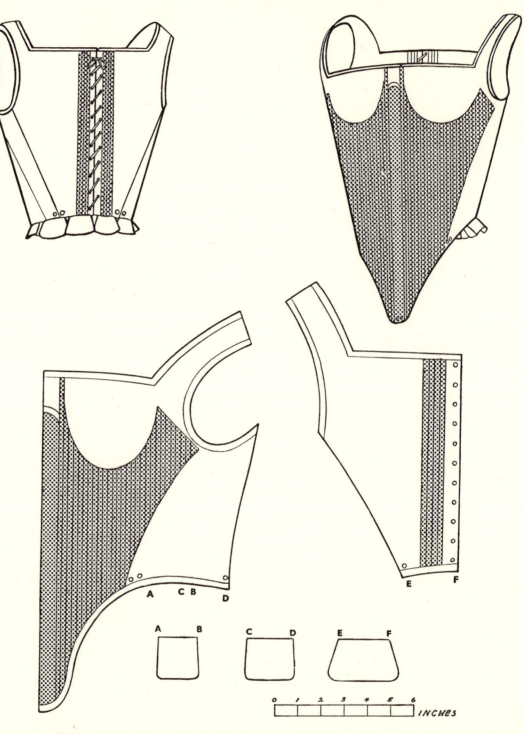

2. Body of yellow-brown silk, edged with silk ribbon; the lining, probably of linen, has perished; the whalebone or other stiffening used has also perished, but the stitching—back-stitch in silk—remains to show where it had been inserted; the centre front would have had a broad busk—wood, whalebone, or horn. The eyelet holes are stitched over iron rings, those round the waist for the laces tying the body to the petticoat or farthingale, the two centre front for the busk lace (*early seventeenth century*)

they began to call it a "waistcoat". This waistcoat was made of two or more layers of heavy linen, quilted together and often padded, and usually with a short basque provided with eyelet holes to which the hose were laced; at the end of the fifteenth century it was the fashion to wear the outer robe open, and consequently the fore part of this waistcoat began to be richly embroidered and jewelled, laced up the sides, or, if laced or fastened in front, an extra decorated piece was worn to hide these fastenings: this was the "stomacher" or "placard". When the women began to wear this garment they called it a "pair of bodys", sometimes just "body", though "body" was more usually applied to the upper part of the outer robe. The French used this same word *corps* for both upper- and under-bodice, and it was always in the singular.

This early form of "corset" was probably quite simple in shape; it would be made from two pieces of linen (sometimes stiffened by paste), stitched together and shaped to the waist at the sides. To keep the front part really rigid a "busc" was added. This was a piece of wood, horn, whalebone, metal, or ivory, usually thicker at the top and tapering towards the point, often beautifully decorated; it was inserted between the layers of linen of the fore part of the body and tied there by a lace. The busc could easily be removed, and the "busc-lace" was frequently worn by the gallants of the period tied round the arm, or to their hat band, as sign of their lady's favour. In the second half of the century the pair of bodys was further reinforced by adding whalebones to the sides and back; the side lacing of the early period was changed to the more convenient centre back or front opening (2). When gowns open in front became fashionable the "stomacher" piece would be added to disguise a centre front lacing.

In the next century the "pair of bodys" was called a "pair of stays", a name which has been used down to the present century to denote any under-bodice with artificial supports or stays. In England the word "corset" may occasionally be seen from the seventeenth century onwards, but it is always used in the plural, or a "pair of stays". France retained the old form *corps* until the end of the eighteenth century; after that "corset", always in the singular, is used.

The fashions at the beginning of the seventeenth century were very similar in shape to those worn at the end of the previous one. The neckline became much lower in front and about 1620, after the farthingale was finally discarded, the body of the gown was worn much shorter. The stays followed the fashionable waistline but kept the long centre front stomacher, and the basque was replaced by long side-tabs, to which the full petticoats were still tied. In the portraits of the period these stays, covered with rich material, can easily be seen worn under the long, open robe. A short bodice, with tabs, like the man's doublet of the same period, appeared about 1630, and was worn throughout the middle of the seventeenth century, and by the bourgeoisie and lower classes long after the woman of fashion had discarded it; it was either boned or worn over a separate pair of stays (3).

During the seventeenth century a softer, more rounded silhouette was gradually coming in; the stiff, patterned brocades and velvets were replaced by simpler materials. It must be remembered that the best silks, velvets, brocades, laces, etc., still came from Italy. In England the Civil War and the coming to power of the Puritan regime put an end to extravagance in dress; in France the import of foreign merchandise had reached such a scale that edicts had to be passed prohibiting the wearing of such goods, with the result

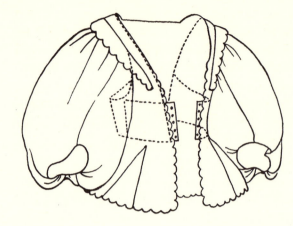
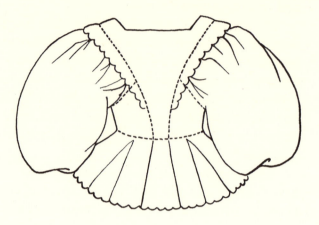

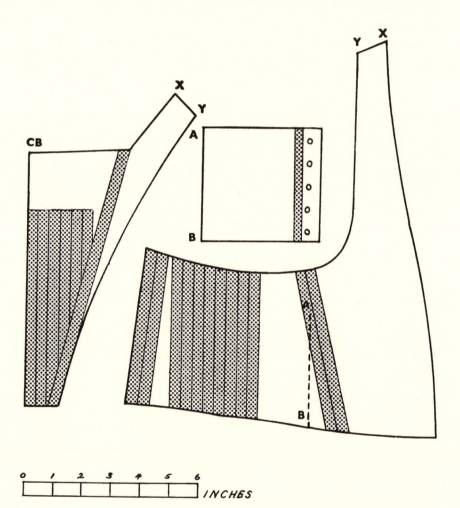

3. White satin bodice with basque and large sleeves. The short body only (*see pattern*) is mounted on a stiff inter-lining made from two layers of stiffened linen, between which are inserted very thin strips of whale bone (*c. 1630*)

0 1 2 3 4 5 6 INCHES

that the French home-produced silks, simpler in design and inferior in quality, were worn and created a new fashion.

In the late thirties the fashionable Englishwoman favoured a very simple style of dress; it had a very low-necked and short-waisted body, without tabs, full skirts, and large, unstiffened sleeves. As the whole silhouette became longer and straighter stays almost disappeared and, in fact, became incorporated into the gown itself, the body of which was now mounted on a stiff, whaleboned lining. In the forties the waist began to descend again, but the simple style of gown remained in fashion, the body being still fashioned on the heavily whaleboned, stay-like foundation. Similar boned bodices were also worn on the Continent.

Shoulder-straps are an essential part of the whaleboned stays, the stiff body of which is not shaped to the breasts; consequently the straps are necessary to hold the stays in place and force the breasts upwards. Throughout the sixteenth century the shoulder-straps were right on the shoulders, but during the seventeenth century they gradually slipped off to the top of the arm, and by the middle of the century were right off the shoulder, across the top of the arm, thus producing the oval neckline so typical of the period.

It is regrettable that few garments of any kind of this period have survived. The earliest specimens of stays are the iron ones, dating from the end of the sixteenth and the beginning of the seventeenth century. They are generally made from four plates of iron, decorated with ornamental perforations, hinged at the sides and centre front, and usually have the opening centre back. They appear to have formerly had a padded lining. As contemporary texts usually refer to whaleboned "bodys" only, these iron ones are now regarded as orthopaedic instruments. They are beautifully designed and very elegant in shape (4, 5).

THE FARTHINGALE

THE earliest references to a farthingale are to be found in Spanish texts, and the first contemporary representation of a woman's skirt obviously artificially extended is also Spanish. They both belong to the end of the fifteenth century. The name also is of Spanish origin, being derived from *verdugos*, saplings, probably because they were used to construct these early hoop petticoats; later cane and whalebone took their place (1).

The farthingale seems to have reached England early in the sixteenth century; the somewhat erratic English spelling of the period varied considerably—vardingal, fardyngale, verthingale, etc., before finally settling for "farthingale".

The Spanish farthingale was cone-shaped, a series of graduated hoops giving the required shape. Though this form was worn in England and France until about the middle of the sixteenth century, it is obvious from portraits of the period that an extra padding had been added to the hips to give them a more rounded shape. In the second half of the century this padded roll had grown in favour and size, it was called the "French farthingale", *hausse-cul*, and eventually replaced the stiffer Spanish one (6, 7, 9).

Towards the end of the sixteenth century, when distortion of shape in both men's and women's costume reached its peak, the padded roll became so large and cumbersome that cane or whalebone was again used in the petticoat; this time it was placed high in the skirt on a level with the waistline, pleats radiating from the waist kept it in position, and the long busc point of the boned body which rested on the edge of this frame produced the fashionable tilt. It was usually narrower in front than at the back. From its shape it was known as the "wheel farthingale". This shape may also have been produced by a wheel-like extension of the basque of the boned body, either stitched to it at the waist or attached there by laces (8). This wheel farthingale was worn until about 1620, though portraits showing a simpler type of dress, without a farthingale, are common in England from a much earlier date. The padded roll never entirely disappeared; it became much smaller and may be seen down to about 1640. The very slender line of this century, however, was of such short duration that some form of padded roll or a pair of hip-pads must usually have been worn to give the skirts their correct hang.

Spain retained the cone-shaped farthingale until well into the seventeenth century, when it began to flatten front and back and extend on either side. This later shape is usually known as *garde-infante* and can be seen in the Velasquez portraits.

REFERENCES TO WHALEBONED BODIES AND FARTHINGALES FROM CONTEMPORARY SOURCES

Fourteenth Century

Ther kerteles were of rede sandel;
I lascid small, joliff, and well.
There might none gayer go

The lady was clad in purple pall
With gentill bodye and middle small.
Quoted by JOSEPH STRUTT, *Dress and Habits of the People of England*

1477

There is another dress which is very ugly, for it makes women appear very fat and as wide as tongues. It is true that by nature women should be short, with slender or narrow shoulders, breasts and back, and small heads, and that their faces should be thin and small . . . and also that they should be wide and big round the back and belly and hips so that they can have space for the children they conceive and carry for nine months. . . . But although this is true, the aforesaid dress greatly exceeds and more than greatly exceeds, the natural proportions, and instead of making woman beautiful and well-proportioned, makes them ugly, monstrous and deformed until they cease to look like women and look like bells. . . . Finally, such dress is very deceitful and very ugly. It is in truth great deceit in a woman who is slender, hipless, and very thin, to give herself hips and a shape with cloth and wool; if carried out in moderation it might be overlooked and at most would be a venial sin. But done in such a way, without moderation and with exaggeration, it is undoubtedly a deception and a lie of great guilt and consequently a great sin. . . . Thus it is a sin when women who are small of stature wear chopines to feign a height they do not possess, especially as Our Lord has willed it that women are usually short of body and smaller than men, since they have to be ruled by them as their superiors, or when they with rags, wool, petticoats or hoops, affect a width which they do not possess. There is no doubt that deception and lies are a mortal sin when carried out in the above evil and sinful manner; thus the padded hips and hoop skirts are very harmful and very wicked garments; with reason they have been forbidden under pain of excommunication.

MSS. FRAY FERNANDO OF TALAVERA: quoted in *Soc. Española de Excursiones*, Bol. XII

1470

Par détestable vanité, les femmes d'estat font faire leurs robes si estroites par le faux du corps que à peine peuvent elles dedans respirer et souventes fois grant doleur y souffrent pour faire gent le corps menu.
PIERRE DES GROS, *Jardin des Nobles*

1505   *Memorials of King Henry VII*

Instructions given by the King's Highness to his trusty and well beloved servants, Francis Marsin, James Braybroke, and John Stile, showing how they shall order themselves when they shall come to the presence of the old Queen of Naples and the young Queen her daughter . . .

16 Item, to mark her breasts and paps, whether they be big or small.

As to this article, the said Queen's breasts be somewhat great and fully, and inasmuch as that they were trussed somewhat high, after the manner of the country, the which causeth her grace for to seem much the fullyer and her neck to be the shorter.

Quoted by G. G. COULTON, *Life in the Middle Ages*, Vol. III

1519

The Kyng, on the vii daie of Marche prepared a disguysyng, and caused his greate chamber at Grenewiche to be staged. . . . Into this chamber came the kyng and quene, there was a goodly commedy of Plautus plaied, and that done, there entred into the chamber eight ladies in blacke velvet bordred about with gold, with hoopes from the wast douneward, and sleves ruffed and plited at the elbowe and plain in the middes, full of cuttes, plucked out at every cutte with fine Camericke, and tired like to the Egipcians very richly.

HALL'S *Chronicles*

1519

One waistcoat of cloth of silver quilted with black silk and tufted out with fine "camerike".
White satin waistcoat, the sleeves embroidered with Venice silver.
Half a yard for the king's placard or stomacher.
Placard of purple cloth of tissue, raised with flowers of gold, edged with sables.

Quoted by JOSEPH STRUTT, *Dress and Habits of the People of England*

1551 L.R. 2/119

Stomacher of black vellet embroidered with purles.

1578

Itm for making of foure stomachers of paste bourde covered with taphata.

1545

vii virg. Satten de bruges crimsen pro una verdingale—Princess Elizabeth.

1560

5 yds. purple taffeta for farthingale, 7¾ yds. purple velvet for border, 7½ yds. kersey for the ropes (casings).

1566

To John Bate, "verthingale maker", payment for a farthingale of "crymsen tuft taffeta edged cum crymsen vellat" also for a hamper to carry "two verthingales in".

1587/9

157 yards of whalebone for three farthingales, 214 yards for seven farthingales.

Quoted by M. C. LINTHICUM, *Costume in Elizabethan Drama*

1532/5

Next to the smock they put on the pretty kirtle or vasquin of pure silk chamelot; above that went the taffatie or tabi vardingale, of white, red, tanne, gray or any other colour; above this taffatie petticoat they had another of cloth of tissue or brocade, embroidered with fine gold, and interlaced with needle-work or as they thought good.

FRANÇOIS RABELAIS, *Gargantua*

1550

Hyr mydle braced in,
  as smal as a wande;
And some by wastes of wyre
  at the paste wyfes hand.

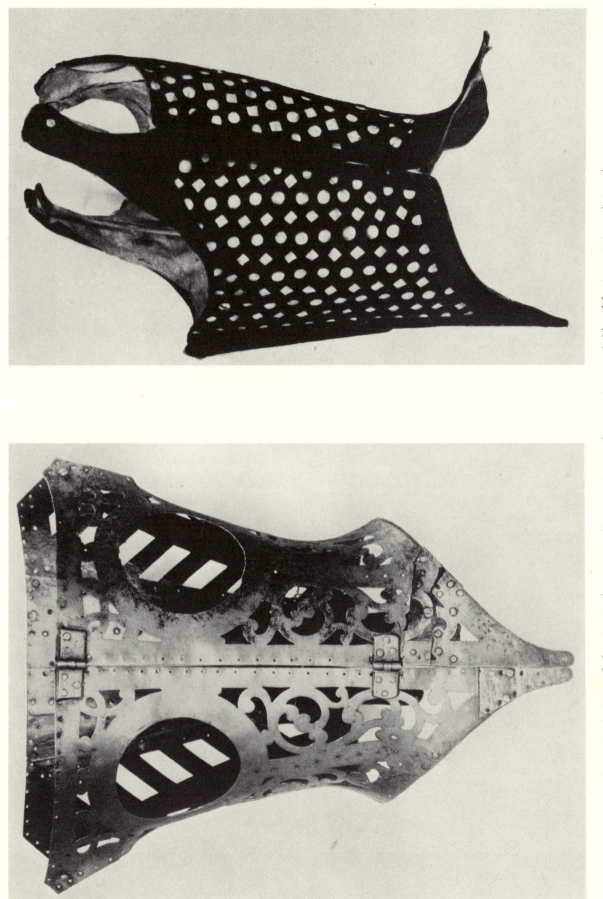

4, 5 **Beginning of the sixteenth century.** Two specimens of iron corsets, probably of foreign origin or designed for difficult or deformed figures. "Whaleboned bodys" were more generally worn in England and France

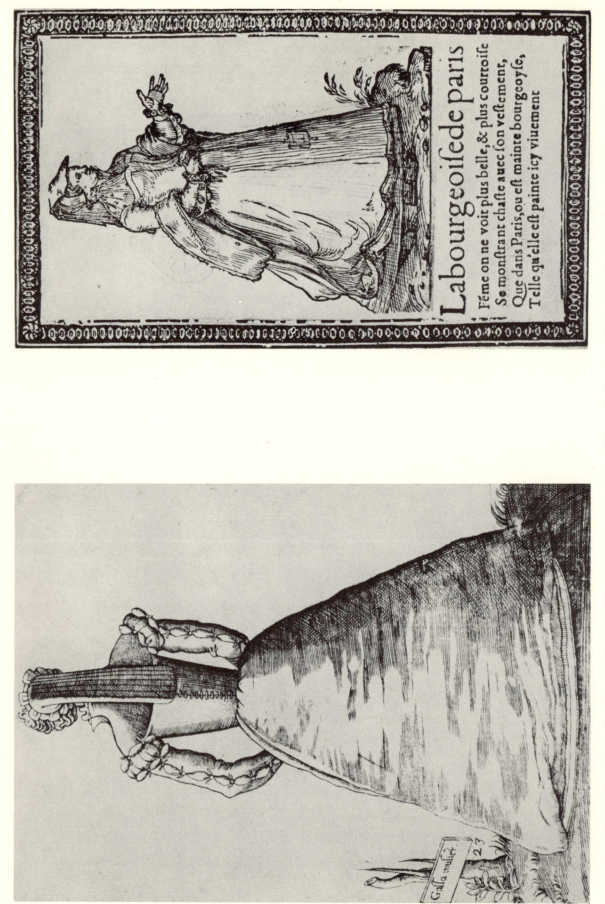

6, 7 Sixteenth century. The bottom of the whaleboned or caned petticoat, the "Spanish Farthingale", is just visible under the skirts of the two dresses

From "Receuil de la Diversite des Habits", 1567

From Ferdinando Bertelli, "Omnium fere gentium nostrae aetatis habitus", 1563

A bumbe lyke a barrell,
with whoopes at the skyrte,
Hyr shoes of such stuffe
that may touche no dyrte.

ROBERT CROWLEY, *One and Thyrtye Epigrammes*

1559

Ordre du duc d'albe espousant Elisabeth de France, fille aisnée du roy Henre II, comme procureur du Philippe II, roy d'espagne, en l'église Nostre-Dame de Paris, l'an 1559, au mois de juin.

Une verdugade couverte de camelot d'or violet.
Une couverture de vertugade, pour tous les jours,
de damas violet avec du passement autour, large, a jour.

DUC DE GUISE, *Mémoires-Journaux*

1562

Alas poor verdingales must lie in the streete,
To house them no doore in the citee made meete,
Syns at our narrow doores they in can not win,
Send them to Oxforde, at Brodegates to get in.

JOHN HEYWOOD, *Epigrams*

1563

Laissez ces vilaines basquines
Qui vous font laides comme quines
Vestez vous comme prudes femmes
Sans plus porter ces busqs infames.

La vertugalle nous aurons,
Maulgré eulx et leur faulse envie,
Et le busque au sein porterons;
N'est-ce pas usance jolye?

Quoted by A. DE LA FIZELIÈRE, *L'Histoire de la Crinoline au temps passé*

1577

French women have inconceivably narrow waists; they swell out their gowns from the waist downwards by whaleboned stuffs and vertugadins, which increases the elegance of their figures. Over the chemise they wear a corset or bodice, that they call a "corps piqué" which makes their shape more delicate and more slender. It is fastened behind which helps to show off the form of the bust.

JÉRÔME LIPPOMANO, *Voyage de Jérôme Lippomano, ambassadeur de Venise en France en* 1577

1588

"In viero, tres amoris onciae, in femina, nouem." In a man three ounces of lust, in a woman nine; for what meaneth els their outward tricking and daintie trimming of their heads, the laying out of their hayres, the painting and washing of their faces, the opening of their breasts, and discovering them to their wastes, their bentes of whale bone to beare out their bummes, their great sleeves and bumbasted shoulders, squared in breadth to make their wastes small, their culloured hose, their variable shooes? And all these are but outward showes.

WILLIAM AVERELL, *A Mervailous Combat of Contrarieties*

1588

To become slender in wast, and to have a straight spagnolised body, what pinching, what girding, what cingling, will they not endure; yea sometimes with yron-plates, with whale-bones and other such trash, that their very skin, and quicke flesh is eaten and consumed to the bones; whereby they sometimes worke their own death.

All high and more than human Sciences are decked and enrobed with Poeticall stile. Even as women . . . make trunk-sleeves of wyre, and whale-bone bodices, backes of lathes, and stiffe bumbasted verdugals, and, to the open-view of all men, paint and embellish themselves with counterfeit and borrowed beauties, so doth learning.

MONTAIGNE, *Essayes . . . now done into English by John Florio* 1603

1589

> But heard you nam'd,
> Till now of late, Busks, Perrewigs, Maskes, Plumes of feathers fram'd;
> Supporters, Pooters, Fardingales, above the Loynes to waire,
> That be she near so bombe-thin, yet she crosse like seems four squaire.

WILLIAM WARNER, *Albion's England*

1591   *Bower of Delights*

He puts on his armour over his ears, like a waistcoat.

NICHOLAS BRETON: quoted by M. C. LINTHICUM, *Costume in Elizabethan Drama*

1596

> These privie coates, by art made strong
>   with bones, with past, with such like ware
> Whereby their backe and sides grow long,
>   and now they harnest gallants are;
>   Were they for use against the foe,
>   Our dames for Amazones mught goe.
>
> But seeing they doe only stay
>   the course that nature doth intend,
> And mothers often by them slay
>   their daughters yoong, and worke their end,
>   What are they els but armours stout,
>   Wherein like gyants, Jove they flout?
>
> These hoopes, that hippes and haunch do hide,
>   and heave aloft the gay hoist traine,
> As they are now in use for pride,
>   so did they first beginne of paine;
>   When whores in stewes had gotten poxe,
>   The French device kept coats from smocks.

STEPHEN GOSSON, *Pleasant Quippes for Upstart New-Fangled Gentlewomen*

1597

I will have a petitcoat of silk, not red, but of the best silk that is; it shall be guarded and a foot high; it shall be laid on with gold lace; it shall have a French bodys not of whalebone for that is not stiff enough, but of horn for that will hold it out; it shall come low before to keep in my belly. My lad, I will have a French fardingale, it shall be finer than thine; I will have it low before and high behind, and broad on either side, that I may lay my arms upon it. . . . I will have a busk of whalebone, it shall be tied with two silk points, and I will have a drawn wrought stomacher embossed with gold.

Quoted by G. B. HARRISON, *Elizabethan Journal*

1597

Layd out for the company of my lord admeralles men for to by tafetie tinsell to make a payr of bodyes for a womanes gowne to playe allece perce in . . . . xx.s.

PHILIP HENSLOWE, *Diary*

1599

English burgher women usually wear high hats covered with velvet or silk for headgear, with cut-away kirtles when they go out, in the old-fashioned style. Instead of whalebone they wear a broad circular piece of wood over the breast to keep the body straighter and more erect. English women of the nobility dress very similarly to the French except for very long stomachers.

THOMAS PLATTER, *Travels in England* 1599

1602

Secretary Scaramelli sees Queen Elizabeth—The Queen wore a dress of silver and white tabi edged with bullion, and rather open in front, so as to display the throat, enriched with pearls and rubies mid-way down the breast; the swell of her gown was much greater than is the fashion in France; and descended lower; her head-dress being of fair hair, such as nature could not have produced.

Venetian Calendar, Vol. IX

1602

CHLOE: Alas, man, there was not a gentleman came to your house in your t'other wife's time, I hope! Nor a lady, nor music, nor masques! Nor you nor your house were so much as spoken of, before I disbased myself, from my hood, and my farthingal, to these bum-rowls and your whale-bone bodice.

BEN JONSON, *The Poetaster*

1605

Germany—and in many Cities, aswel the married as unmarried Women, weare long fardingales, hanging about their feete like hoopes, which our Women used of olde, but have now changed to short fardingals about their hippes.

FYNES MORYSON, *An Itinerary*

1605

Goe fetch my cloathes: bring my petty-coate bodyes: I meane my damask quilt bodies with whale bones: what lace doe you give me heere? this lace is too shorte, the tagges are broken, I cannot lace my selfe with it, take it away, I will have that of greene silke.

PIERRE ERONDELLE, *The French Garden*

1608

> *"Ladies' Favours"*
> Lord, when I thinke, what a paltry thing
>   Is a glove, or a ring,
> Or a top of a fan, to brag of:
> And how much a noddy
>   Will triumph in a buske point,
> Snatch'd with the tagge of;
> Then I say,
>   Well fare him,
> That hath ever used close play.
>   Quoted by F. W. FAIRHOLT, *Satirical Songs and Poems on Costume*

1608

> *"Panegyrick Verses"*
> On th'other side the Round stands one as tall too,
> Drest like a French-fem, in a farthingall too,
> Upholding (as the other did) the Rundle,
> Whose clothes, about the Bumme, tuckt like a bundle
>   Doe make her stand for France; and so she may well,
>   For shee hath Stuffe to make her Doo and say well.
>   THOMAS CORYATE, *Crudities*

1611

BALENES: Whall-bones; whall-bone bodies; French bodies.
BASQUINE: A Vardingall of the old Fashion or a Spanish Vardingall.
BUC: A buske, plated body, or other quilted thing, worn to make, or keep, the body straight.
CORSET: A little body, also a paire of bodies (for a woman).
HAUSSE-CUL: A French Vardingale or (more properly) the kind of roll used by such women, as weare
  (or are to weare) no Vardingales.
VERTUGALLE: A Vardingale.

RANDLE COTGRAVE, *A French-English Dictionary*

1613

"Le Discours sur la Mode"
Le grand vertugadin est commun aux Françoises,
Dont usent maintenant librement les bourgeoises,
Tout de mesme que font les dames, si ce n'est
Qu'avec un plus petit la bourgeoise paroist;
Car les dames ne sont pas bien accommodées
Si leur vertugadin n'est large dix coudées.

Quoted by A. DE LA FIZELIÈRE, *L'Histoire de la Crinoline au temps passé*

Beginning of the Seventeenth Century

La Reine Marguerite de Valois—Elle portoit un grand vertugadin, qui avoit des pochettes tout
autour, en chacune desquelles elle mettoit une boîte où étoit le cœur d'un de ses amants trépassés; car
elle étoit soigneuse, à mesure qu'ils mouroient, d'en faire embaumer le cœur. Ce vertugadin se pendoit
tous les soirs à un crochet, qui fermoit à cadenas, derrière le dossier de son lit. . . . Elle devint horriblement grosse, et avec cela elle faisoit faire ses carrures et ses corps de jupes beaucoup plus larges qu'il
ne le failloit, et ses manches à proportion . . . pour se rendre de plus belle taille, elle faisoit mettre du
ferblanc aux deux côtés de son corps pour élargir la carrure. Il y avoit bien des portes où elle ne pouvoit
passer.
  Madame de Gondron—Elle se serroit tellement pour paroître de belle taille, qu'elle se blessa si fort
au côté qu'il s'y fit un trou.

TALLEMANT DES RÉAUX, *Les Historiettes*

Beginning of the Seventeenth Century

When Sir Peter Wych was Embassadour to the Grand Signeour from King James, his Lady being
then with him at Constantinople, the Sultanesse desired one day to see his Lady, whom she had heard
much of; whereupon my Lady Wych (accompanied by her waiting-women, all neatly dressed in their
great Verdingals, which was the Court Fashion then) attended her Highnesse. The Sultanesse entertained
her respectfully, but withall wondring at her great and spacious Hips, she asked her whether all English
women were so made and shaped about those parts; To which my Lady Wych answered, that they
were made as other women were, withall shewing the fallacy of her apparell in the device of the Verdin-
gall untill which demonstration was made, the Sultanesse verily believed it had been her naturall and
reall shape.
JOHN BULWER, *The Pedigree of the English Gallant*

1612

One thing I had almost forgotten, that all this time, there was a course taken, and so notified, that
no lady or gentleman should be admitted to any of these sights with a vardingale, which gain the
more room, and I hope may serve to make them quite left off in time.

1617

My Lady Bennet would not vouchsafe, all the while she was in Holland, nor yet on going or coming
to Amsterdam, to visit the Hague; but she had seen enough of that good town, though she was in a

8 **1615.** Costumes designed for a ballet, *Les Esperducattis*, suggesting that the "Wheel Farthingale" may have been produced by attaching a whaleboned frame to the basque of the "boned body"

9 ***c.* 1600.** "Hausse-cul: a French Vardingale or the kind of roll used by such women as weare no Vardingales"

From a contemporary Dutch caricature

10 *c.* **1650–1660.** Boned
bodice of blue moiré
silk. The construction
of the foundation of
this bodice is shown
in Fig. 12

The London Museum

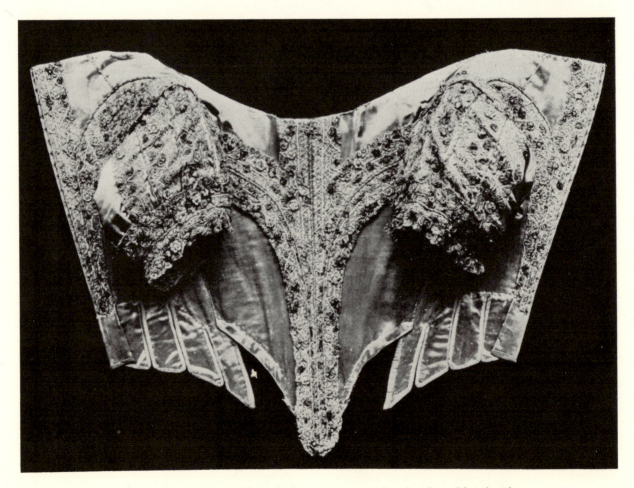

11 *c.* **1660.** Boned bodice of white satin, trimmed with coloured lace braid

The Victoria and Albert Museum

nest of hornets, as she told her friends and kindred, by reason of the boys and wenches, who much wondered at her huge farthingales and fine gowns, and saluted her at every turn of the street with their usual caresses of "Hoore! hoore!" And she was more exposed to view, because, when she would go closely in a covered wagon about the town, she could not, because there was no possible means to hide half her farthingale. THOMAS BIRCH, *The Court and Times of James I*

1617

Audience of Venetian Ambassador with Queen Anne of Denmark—Her Majesty's costume was pink and gold with so expansive a farthingale that I do not exaggerate when I say it was four feet wide in the hips; her bosom was bare down to the pit of the stomach, forming as it were, an oval.
Venetian Calendar, Vol. XV

1617

> Else (mincing madams) why do we (alas!)
> Pine at your Pencill and conspiring Glasse?
> Your Curles, Purles, Perriwigs, your Whale bone wheels?
> That shelter all defects from head to heeles.
> HENRY FITZ-JEOFFERY, *Satyres and Satyrical Epigrams*

1617

November—All the time I was at the Court I wore my green damask gown embroidered without a farthingale.

The 28th was the first time the Child put on a pair of whale bone bodice. (The Child—Lady Margaret Sackville, b. 1614.) LADY ANNE CLIFFORD, *Diary*

1617

BODIE: A pair of Bodies for a Woman—Fr. Corpset, corset.
BUSKE: Made of wood or whale-bone, a plated or quilted thing to keep the body straight.
JOHN MINSHEU, *The Guide into Tongues*

Middle of the Seventeenth Century
Verses engraved on a busk worn by Anne of Austria:

> Ma place ordinairement
> Est sur le cœur de ma maîtresse,
> D'où j'ouis soupirer un amant
> Qui voudrait bien tenir ma place.
> Quoted by ERNEST LÉOTY, *Le Corset à travers les Âges*

1650

Another foolish affection there is in young Virgins, though grown big enough to be wiser, but that they are led blindfold by custome to a fashion pernitious beyond imagination; who thinking a Slender-Waste a great beauty, strive all that they possibly can by streight-lacing themselves, to attain unto a wand-like smalnesse of Waste, never thinking themselves fine enough untill they can span their Waste. By which deadly artifice they reduce their Breasts into such streights, that they soon purchase a stinking breath; and while they ignorantly affect an august or narrow Breast, and to that end by strong compulsion shut up their Wastes in a Whale-bone prison or little-ease, they open a door to Consumptions, and a withering rottennesse. JOHN BULWER, *The Artificial Changeling*

1660

Mariage de Louis XIV à l'Infante—L'habit et la coiffure des femmes d'Espagne me fit de la peine à voir. Leur corps n'étoit point vêtu de rien qui fût ferme, et leur gorgette étoit ouverte par derrière. . . . Leur guard-Infante étoit une machine à demi ronde et monstreuse, car il sembloit que c'étoient plusieurs cercles de tonneau cousus en dedans de leurs jupes, hormis que les cercles sont ronds, et que leur guard-Infante étoit aplati un peu par devant et par derrière, et s'élargissoit par les côtés. Quand elles marchoient cette machine se haussoit et se baissoit, et faisoit enfin une forte laide figure. . . . On fit voir à la Reine ses habits, son linge, ses toilettes et les choses nécessaires à la noce, qui avoient été mises en reserve en ce lieu . . . Le soir on lui essaya ses habits à la française, et on lui mit pour la première fois un corps de jupe. . . . Elle en fut d'abord incommodée mais le souffrit avec douceur et patience.

MME DE MOTTEVILLE, *Mémoires pour servir à l'histoire d'Anne d'Autriche*

1663

October 30th—At my periwigg-maker's, and there showed my wife the periwigg made for me, and she likes it very well, and so to my brothers, and to buy a pair of boddice for her.

SAMUEL PEPYS, *Diary*

1670

Genoa—The great ladies go in guard infantas (child preservers), that is, in horrible overgrown vertigals of whalebone, which being put about the waist of the lady, and full as broad on both sides as she can reach with the hands, bear out her coats in such a manner that she appears to be as broad as long.

R. LASSELS, *The Voyage of Italy*

1680

BEARERS, ROWLS, FARDINGALES: these are things made purposely to put under skirts of Gowns at their setting on at the Bodies; which raise up the skirt at that place to what breadth the wearer pleaseth, and as the fashion is.

RANDLE HOLME, *The Academy of Armory*

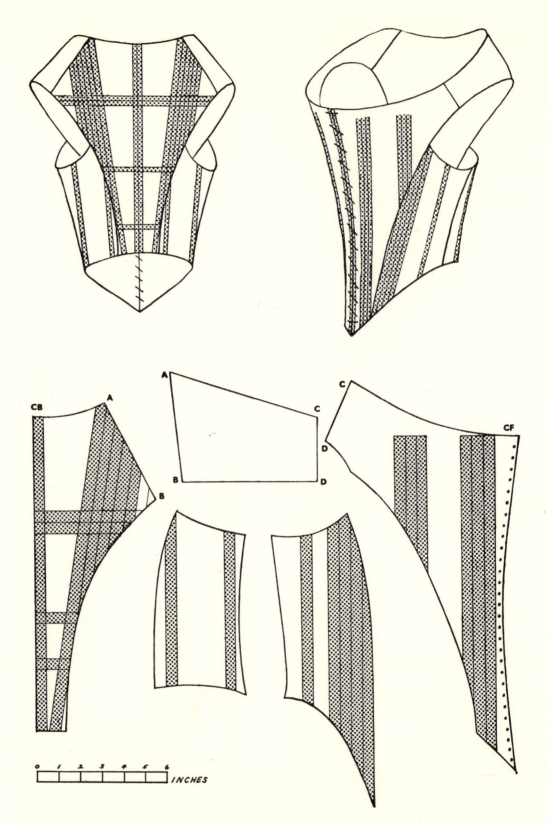

12. Boned lining of a bodice which is covered in pale-blue moiré silk, the seams of which do not correspond with the lining, being narrower and more subtle in shape. The centre front lacing is concealed. This bodice has large elbow-length sleeves with cuffs sewn into the arm hole with fine pleating on the shoulders. It has also a basque made of twenty-eight small tassets sewn together (*1650–1660*)

CHAPTER II

1670 to the End of the Eighteenth Century

1

THE STAYS

WHAT are usually referred to as eighteenth-century corsets are the stays that had their origin in the boned bodice of the middle of the seventeenth century. This bodice reached the waist about 1650 and went on descending. This was achieved by lengthening the centre front and centre back pieces; the sides, too, extended down over the hips, where they were slit up to the waistline and so formed tabs which spread out to allow for the roundness of the hips; the whalebone being carried down the tabs which prevented it from digging into the body at the waist. The bodice had now acquired side front seams which ran from the armhole diagonally almost down to the point of the busc, and behind from the armhole almost to the centre back at the waist line; the whalebone was inserted straight at the under arm, but fanned out to follow the side front and side back seams. This arrangement gave a more rounded shape and consequently a more slender appearance to the body, which from the wide oval neckline seemed to taper down to nothing. The centre front seam was often curved and the busc followed this shaping. This bodice foundation was still made of two layers of heavy linen, or canvas, often stiffened with paste or glue, the whalebones inserted between being kept in position by long rows of stitching. It usually laced up centre back, but sometimes also centre front. It was either fully boned (*baleiné*) or half-boned (*demi-baleiné*). The covering material was then stretched over this foundation, the seams not necessarily corresponding; sleeves were attached (10, 12). This bodice was worn, by the fashionable, with the long centre front outside the skirt of the dress, but the side and back tabs went under it; these were sometimes provided with small loops to which the skirts could be hooked in order to keep them in position (11).

In the 1670's the over-robe style of gown came into favour and consequently the boned bodice, worn under it, became again the stays. The stays had by now been recognised as an essential part of a lady's toilette, and the staymaker (*tailleur de corps baleiné*) separated from the habit-maker and became a specialist in his own particular line.

The long narrow lines of the architecture and furniture of the end of the seventeenth century were repeated in the fashionable clothes—i.e. the high "Fontanges" headdress, the narrow body, and the long train. A slender line was given to the stays by adding more seams, which straightened out and tapered down to the waistline, and the whalebones were inserted at subtle angles to give elegance to the otherwise too rigid body; the

37

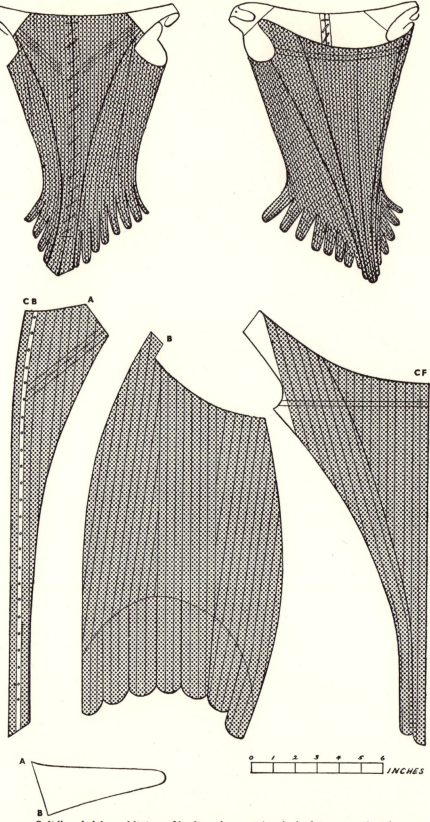

13. Solidly whaleboned lining of bodice, the outside of which is covered with cream satin beautifully embroidered with a floral design in coloured silks and gold and silver; the outside has only the two side seams. Probably the bodice of a court dress, as from about this date the day robes were worn back on the shoulders again. This bodice is very similar in shape to the stays worn by the effigy of the Duchess of Richmond in Westminster Abbey, 1701-1702 (c. 1680)

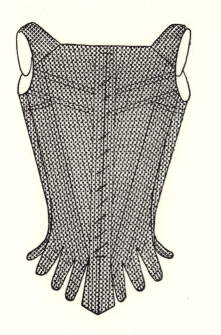
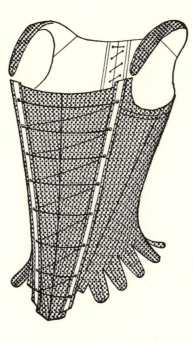

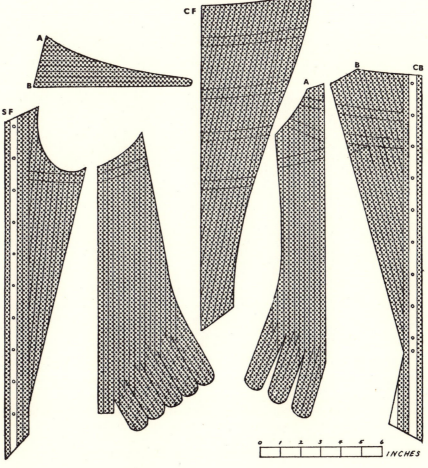

14. Fully-boned stays covered in a very beautiful brocade, yellow with flower design in colours and gold; the stitching comes through the brocade, which is unusual with such a rich covering. It is laced in front, with a separate stomacher (1730–1740)

0 1 2 3 4 5 6 INCHES

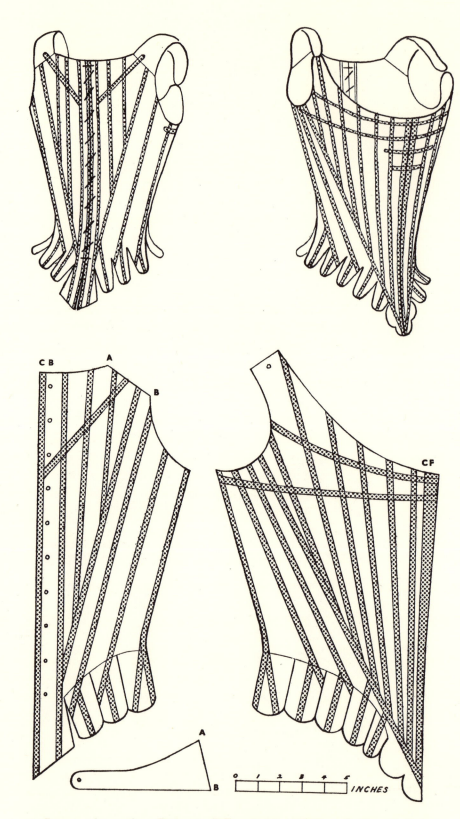

15. Pattern of stays from Diderot's *L'Encyclopédie*, "Tailleur de Corps". It is a half-boned stay, cut from six pieces only, the shaping being given by the direction of the bones. It would have the extra busk and the shaping bones across the front and across the shoulder blades. It might also be fully boned (*1776*)

shoulder pieces went back to the top of the shoulders to continue the narrow line up-wards; they were attached to the back and usually laced to the front and sometimes they too were boned. Stays of this period can be recognised by the number of seams and their still rather coarse finish; they were usually covered with silk, brocade, or embroidery (13, 21, 22).

By the middle of the eighteenth century the technical skill of the staymaker had reached a very high standard. Besides the whalebones inserted in the body of the bodice and the separate centre front busc bone, there were now extra shaping bones arranged inside the stays (*baleines de dressage*); two or more curved pieces, of heavier whalebone, were laid across the top part of the front to give roundness to the bust, and straight pieces across the shoulder blades to keep the back flat. The direction of the boning varied, but it was always laid diagonally on the sides of the front to narrow the body. Throughout the whole period the stays were made either fully boned or half-boned. When fully boned the bones were laid close together and might be as narrow as an eighth of an inch in width. When it is remembered that all the stitching was back-stitch done by hand, and all the whalebone had to be cut into strips—the thickness varying according to its position on the body—one cannot but admire the craftsmanship of these eighteenth-century corsets.

There is variation also in the methods of lacing, centre back, centre front, or both; a side lacing seems to have been used for pregnancy. When laced centre front the opening was left wider at the top and narrowed towards the waist; the stomacher piece was separate and inserted either behind the lacing or fixed to cover it (14). When the gown opened in front to show the stays the lacing was often a feature of the design of the dress; if a stomacher was used it would probably be decorated. The best specimens of stays of the early part of the century have many seams and beautiful workmanship; they are usually covered with silk or brocade, sometimes embroidery. The English body was generally more rigid than the French, which at this period was often distinguished by a more subtle shaping of the seams. It must be remembered that between 1720–1740 the robe *battante* was the fashion in France; this long, loose robe was frequently worn open and showed the stays beneath, which consequently were of as much importance as the dress itself. Stays will also be found covered in cotton, which has been mounted with the foundation pieces so that the stitching is visible from the outside (*corps piqué*).

By the second half of the eighteenth century the staymaker realised that it was mainly the direction of the whalebone and the supporting inside bones which gave the shape to the stays, so from then onwards less seaming was used, the foundation often being cut from six pieces only—two centre front, two centre back, two shoulder straps; this was also made possible by the very much lower neckline of the front, which now stopped at the point of the bust, while the back remained long (15, 16). Stays of this period have fewer seams, and are more usually covered with plain silk or cotton; they are often very stiff and subtle in form, as the finished stays were moulded to shape by pressing with a hot iron (29, 30).

There is also another variation of stays which is often overlooked and that is the boned bodice of the Court dress (*le grand corps* or *le corps de cour*). When the fashions changed about 1680 it was recognised that bare shoulders and a straight fitting corsage were an excellent setting for the many jewels, heavy embroidery, rich brocades, and laces worn for full dress, so the boned gown bodice was retained. The seaming followed the fashionable

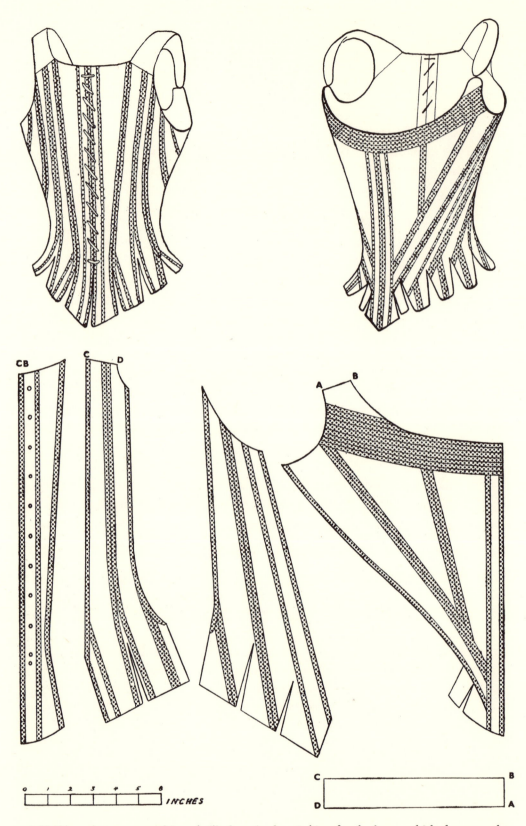

INCHES

16. Half-boned stays, covered in red silk damask, the stitching for the bones which shows on the outside is in white, and the seams are outlined with a narrow white silk ribbon. This shaped stay is often seen fully boned (c. 1780)

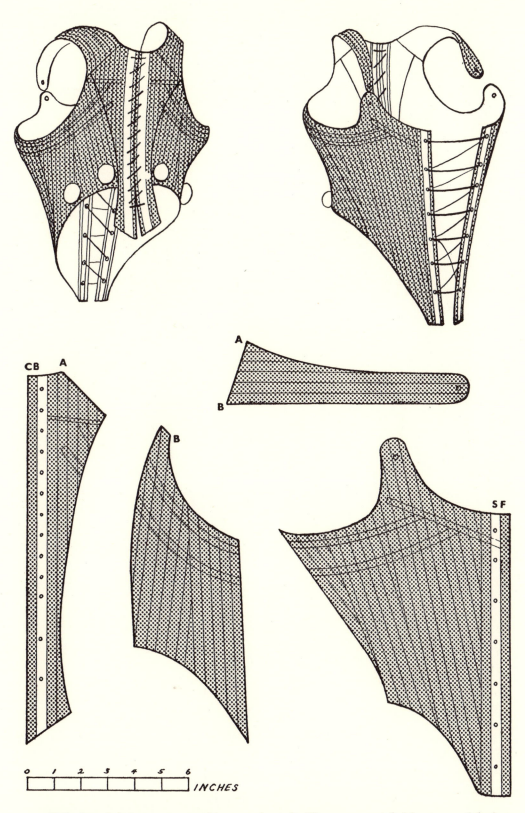

0 1 2 3 4 5 6 INCHES

17. Fully-boned short stays, covered in cream brocade. There are extra whalebones round the large armhole. Petticoats would be attached to the four little padded balls, which make a kind of "bustle" and give the extra fullness to the skirt then fashionable (*c. 1793*)

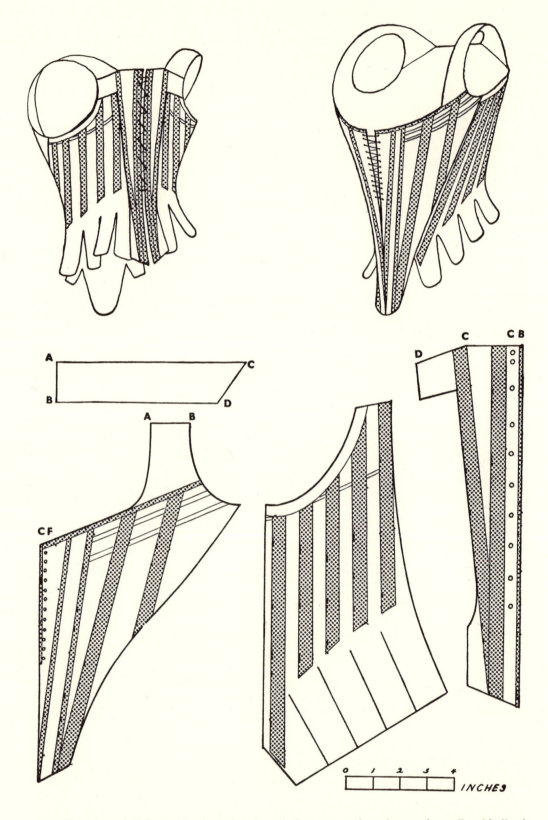

18. Though much lighter and only slightly boned, these stays, of two layers of unstiffened holland, follow on from the previous ones in cut. This type of stay probably continued to be worn in England until well into the next century (*late 1790's*)

line of the moment, but the shoulder straps were always worn off the shoulder. In France, this style of bodice, worn with the enormous panier and train, was obligatory for formal Court wear and remained so until the Revolution. In England we were less rigid, and the very heavily boned bodice with bare shoulders seems to have been reserved for ceremonial occasions only—coronations, royal weddings, etc. Some of the beautifully embroidered stays to be seen in museums may have been originally Court bodices; flounces of beautiful lace would have been used for the sleeves, naturally now missing. It is obvious that the very decorated stays must have been visible because the eighteenth-century craftsman never wasted his art; similarly, those decorated on the front part only would have been worn with an outer robe, open in front. Eighteenth-century stays are always difficult to date and especially those which have obviously been made at home and not by a professional staymaker. When very small they are children's stays, for it was customary to put children—boys as well as girls—into them as soon as they began to walk, in order to give them an upright carriage.

From the end of the seventeenth century printed cottons had been brought to England and France from the East. They became so popular and were so much worn and reproduced that the silk and woollen industries raised a storm of protest. In spite of laws passed prohibiting the printing and wearing of cotton and linen materials they met with no success, and by 1759 in France and 1774 in England all these restrictions had been removed. At first the dresses made from the printed materials were on the lines of the stiff silk ones, but gradually, with increasing use, these softer, hanging cottons began to impose their own style; a looser, more négligé type of dress began to evolve. The simple muslin dresses of the 1780's, with the wide sashes, are well known from the portraits of this period. About 1793 the sash narrowed and brought a high waistline into fashion. With these simpler styles lighter stays began to be worn, at first cut like the previous ones but of less stiff materials, and with fewer bones; as the body of the dress shortened they too began to shrink, the back became even narrower, the front even lower, the tabs began from the high waistline or were discarded altogether (17). They may still be found fully boned, usually half-boned, and sometimes with practically no bones at all (18, 54, 104).

At the end of the century, the chaotic aftermath of the Revolution in France and the worship of the antique style simplified the dress still further. All surplus material was dispensed with and the stays followed suit; they became reduced to a simple band or were discarded altogether. The long reign of the whaleboned body was over.

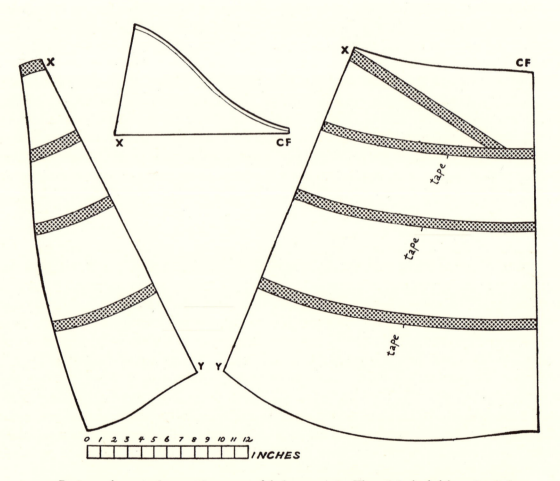

0 1 2 3 4 5 6 7 8 9 10 11 12

INCHES

19. Panier, or hoop petticoat, or improver, of dark green satin. The original whalebone is missing, but the remains of stitching and the marks on the satin clearly indicate where the whalebone had been. The top pieces vary in depth according to the size of the waist (*c. 1740*)

2

THE HOOP PETTICOAT

ONE of the results of the encouragement given to French industry by Louis XIV and his minister Colbert was the great development of the silk trade in France: by the end of the seventeenth century Lyons was producing silks, velvets, brocades, etc., of the most luxurious quality, with rich flowing floral patterns. Woman's dress adapted itself to these new silks, the simple drapery of the earlier style becoming more and more elaborate and the skirts more and more voluminous until finally they required support. At first hip-pads attached to the stays were sufficient; later, at the turn of the century, heavy petticoats, often stiffened with paste or glue, were worn—in France these were known as *criardes*, from the rustling noise they made in movement. Finally came the whaleboned petticoats. England seems to have started this fashion, for it is in English journals dating from 1709 that we first hear of them.

The early form of the hoop petticoat was round and rather dome-shaped; it soon began to flatten back and front, and in spite of all male opposition and raillery it continued to extend on either side until by the middle of the eighteenth century the possible, or rather, impossible, limit of size had been reached. This hoop petticoat, called in France *panier*, and in England sometimes "improver", was usually made of rich material; three or four rows of whalebone were inserted from the waist downward, and extra hoops were laid on the sides to keep them extended. The most elegant French paniers were kidney-shaped and wider round the base (19), whereas the English style was much straighter both in length and breadth (24, 28, 31).

From the middle of the eighteenth century the very large hoop was worn for "full dress" only. Separate small side hoops, often called "pocket hoops", took its place for "undress" and are mentioned as being worn until 1775. These hoops are usually made of cotton (20, 33). For some time the fashionable day dress had been worn caught up and draped over these side hoops, and with the increased use of soft muslins and cottons these too disappeared and the side draperies were carried further to the back; to prop them up and emphasise this new line, a large pad was tied behind. It was frankly called a "bum", or "rump" (*cul postiche*); judging from contemporary references it seems to have frequently been made of cork. This back pad was worn throughout the eighties, and when the waist went up in the nineties it remained, though somewhat smaller, as it prevented the dress from falling into the small of the back at the waistline. These pads are later called "bustles", and may be found well into the next century, as long as the waist remained higher than the normal one (34, 103).

For "full dress", or Court dress (*le grand habit*), the enormous panier was always worn. In France it disappeared with the Revolution. In England, though as a rule we are

47

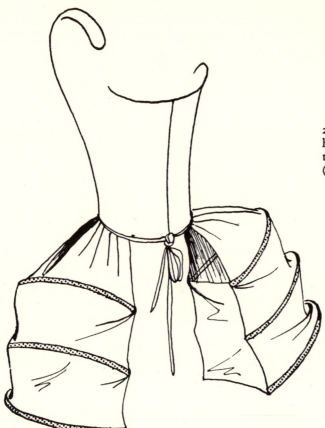

20. Pocket-hoops of striped cotton material; these hoops are separate with a slot round the top through which a tape is put to tie round the waist (c. 1760)

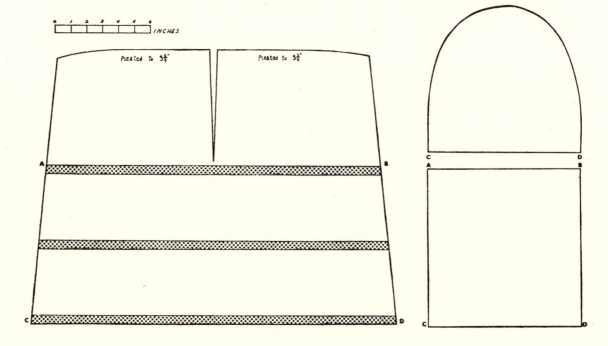

INCHES

Pleated to $3\frac{1}{4}''$ Pleated to $3\frac{1}{4}''$

less conservative and more individual in dress than other countries, this enormous hoop skirt was obligatory for Court dress as late as 1820, when George IV came to the throne. Although we kept the hoop we discarded the long boned body, and the enormous panier appeared in conjunction with the fashionable high-waisted, short-bodied gown—an illogical and ludicrous combination (99).

REFERENCES TO STAYS AND HOOP PETTICOATS FROM CONTEMPORARY SOURCES

1677

À Vichy—Je voudrois que vous vissiez jusqu'à quel excès la présence de Termes et de Flamarens fait monter la coiffure et l'ajustement de deux ou trois belles de ce pays. Enfin dès six heures de matin tout est en l'air, coiffure hurlupée, poudrée, frisée, bonnet à la bascule, rouge, mouches, pettite coiffe qui pend, éventail, corps de jupe long et serré; c'est pour pâmer de rire.

MME DE SÉVIGNÉ, Lettres

1694

They then begin to commit their Body to a close Imprisonment, and pinch it in so narrow a compass, that the best part of its plumpness is forced to rise toward the Neck, to emancipate itself from such hard Captivity; and being proud of her liberty, appears with a kind of pleasant briskness, which becomes her infinitely. As for her fair Breasts, they are half imprisoned, and half free; and do their utmost endeavour to procure their absolute liberty, by shoving back that which veils the one half; but they are too weak to effect it, and whilst they strive to free themselves they cast over a Veil, which perfectly hides them. The desire they have to be expos'd to view, makes them beat it back continually, and not being able to remove that small obstacle, they look quite thro' it: there is nothing constantly free but the upper part of the Neck, which is also more vain-glorious than all the rest, and is adorn'd with a Neck-lace of great value, which adds to its vanity. . . .

Fashion brought in the Vardingale, and carried out the Vardingale, and hath again revived the Vardingale from Death, and placed it behind, like a Rudder or Stern to the body, in some so big, that the Vessel is scarce able to bear it. When God shall come to Judge the quick and the dead, he will not know those who have so defaced that Fashion which he hath Erected.

JOHN DUNTON, Ladies Dictionary

1696

Lettre à la maistresse generale de Saint-Cyr.—Faittes vous donner des mémoires, par les maistresses des classes, qui doivent marquer le temps que les Demoiselles ont esté habillées. Ce n'est pas qu'il faille rien fixer là dessus, car il faut donner aussy souvent des corps, qu'il en sera besoin, pour conserver la taille. Songés au tort que vous faittes à une fille, qui devient bossue par vostre faute, et, par là, hors d'estat de trouver ni mari ni couvent ni dame qui veille s'en charger. N'espargnés rien pour leur âme, pour leur santé, et pour leur taille.

MME. DE MAINTENON, Lettres

1709

December 27th–29th. I have not thoroughly examined their new-fashioned Petticoats, but shall set aside one Day in the next Week for that Purpose.

January 4th, 1710. The Court being prepared for proceedings on the Cause of the Petticoat, I gave Orders to bring in a Criminal who was taken up as she went out of the Puppet-Show about Three Nights ago, and was now standing in the Street with a great Concourse of People about her. Word was brought me, that she had endeavour'd Twice or Thrice to come in, but could not do it by reason of her Petticoat, which was too large for the Entrance of my House, though I had ordered both the Folding-

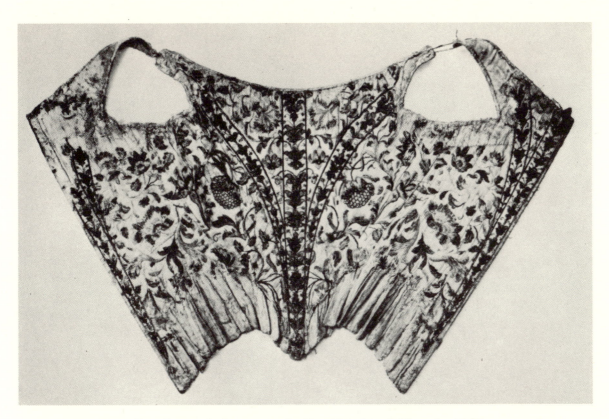

21   *c.* **1690–1700.** "Court" stays of white satin, embroidered in coloured silks and gold. The construction of the foundation of these stays is shown in Fig. 13

The London Museum

22   **1702.** Stays worn by the effigy of the Duchess of Richmond in Westminster Abbey

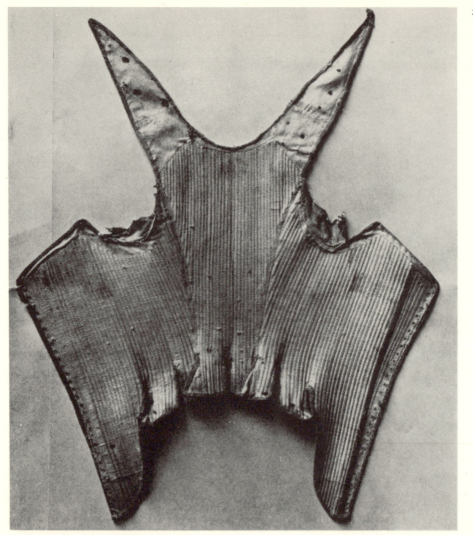

24 **1760.** Panier worn by the effigy of Queen Elizabeth I. It was redressed in 1760

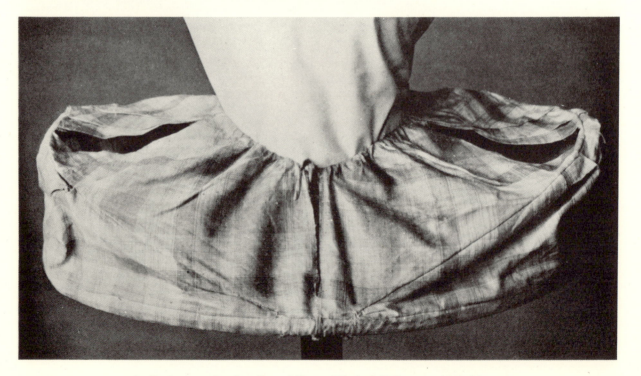

Doors to be thrown open for its Reception. Upon this, I desired the Jury of Matrons, who stood at my Right Hand, to inform themselves of her Condition, and know whether there were any private Reasons why she might not make her Appearance separate from her Petticoat. This was managed with great Discretion, and had such an Effect, that upon the Return of the Verdict from the Bench of Matrons, I issued out an Order forthwith That the Criminal should be stripped of her Incumbrances, till she became little enough to enter my House. I had before given Directions for an Engine of several Legs, that could contract or open itself like the Top of an Umbrello, in order to place the Petticoat upon it, by which Means I might take a leisurely Survey of it, as it should appear in its proper Dimensions. This was all done accordingly; and forthwith, upon the Closing of the Engine the Petticoat was brought into Court. I directed the Machine to be set upon the Table, and dilated in such a manner as to show the Garment in its utmost Circumference; but my great Hall was too narrow for the Experiment; for before it was half unfolded, it described so immoderate a Circle, that the lower Part of it brush'd upon my Face as I sate in my Chair of Judicature. I then enquired for the Person that belonged to the Petticoat, and to my great Surprize, was directed to a very beautiful young Damsel, with so pretty a Face and Shape, that I bid her come out of the Crowd, and seated her upon a little Crock at my Left Hand. "My pretty Maid, (said I) do you own yourself to have been the Inhabitant of the Garment before us?" The Girl I found had good Sense, and told me with a Smile, That notwithstanding it was her own Petticoat, she should be very glad to see an Example made of it: and that she wore it for no other Reason, but that she had a Mind to look as big and burly as other Persons of her Quality; That she had kept out of it as long as she could, and till she began to appear so little in the Eyes of all her Acquaintance; That if she laid it aside, People would think she was not made like other Women. I always give great Allowances to the Fair Sex upon Account of Fashion, and therefore was not displeased with the Defence of my pretty Criminal. I then ordered the Vest which stood before us to be drawn up by a Pulley to the Top of my great Hall, and afterwards to be spread open by the Engine it was placed upon, in such a Manner, that it formed a very splendid and ample Canopy over our Heads, and covered the whole Court of Judicature with a Kind of Silken Rotunda, in its Form not unlike the Cupola of St. Paul's. I enter'd upon the whole Cause with great Satisfaction as I sate under the Shadow of it (26, 28).

The Council for the Petticoat was now called in, and ordered to produce what they had to say against the Popular Cry which was raised against it. . . . The chief Arguments for their Client were taken, first, from the great Benefit that might arise to our Woollen Manufactury from this Invention. . . . To introduce the Second Argument, they begged Leave to read a Petition of the Rope-Makers, wherein it was represented, That the Demand for Cords, and the Price of them, were much risen since this Fashion came up. At this, all the Company who were present lifted up their Eyes into the Vault; and I must confess, we did discover many Traces of Cordage which were interwoven in the Stiffening of the Drapery. A Third Argument was founded upon a Petition of the Greenland Trade, which likewise represented the great Consumption of Whalebone which would be occasioned by the present Fashion, and the Benefit which would thereby accrue to that Branch of the British Trade. To conclude, they gently touched upon the Weight and Unweildiness of the Garment, which they insinuated might be of great Use to preserve the Honour of Families. . . .

I would not be understood, that (while I discard this monstrous Invention) I am an Enemy to the proper Ornaments of the Fair Sex. . . . I would have them bestow upon themselves all the additional Beauties that Art can supply them with, provided it does not interfere with Disguise, or pervert those of Nature . . . every part of Nature shall furnish out its Share towards the Embellishment of a Creature that is the most consummate Work of it. All this I shall indulge them in; but as for the Petticoat I have been speaking of, I neither can, nor will allow it.   *The Tatler*

1711

Mr. Spectator,

You have diverted the Town almost a whole month at the Expense of the Country, it is now high time that you should give the Country their Revenge. Since your withdrawing from this Place, the fair Sex are run into great Extravagancies. Their Petticoats, which began to heave and swell before you left us, are now blown up into a most enormous Concave, and rise every Day more and more; In short, Sir, since our Women know themselves to be out of the Eye of the "Spectator", they will be kept within no Compass. You praised them a little too soon, for the Modesty of their Head-dresses; For as the Humour of a Sick Person is often driven out of one Limb into another, their Superfluity of Ornaments, instead of being entirely Banished, seems only fallen from their Heads upon their Lower Parts. What they have lost in Height they make up in Breadth, and contrary to all Rules of Architecture widen the Foundations at the same time that they shorten the Superstructure. Where they like Spanish Jennets, to impregnate by the Wind, they could not have thought on a more proper Invention. But as we do not yet hear any particular Use in this Petticoat, or that it contains any thing more than what was supposed to be in those of Scantier Make, we are wonderfully at a loss about it.

The Women give out, in Defence of these wide Bottoms, that they are Airy, and very proper for the Season; but this I look upon to be only a Pretence, and a piece of Art, for it is well known we have not had a more moderate Summer these many Years, so that it is certain the Heat they complain of cannot be in the Weather: Besides, I would fain ask these tender-constitutioned Ladies, why they should require more Cooling than their Mothers before them.

I find several Speculative Persons are of Opinion that our Sex has of late Years been very Saucy, and that the Hoop Petticoat is made use of to keep us at a Distance. It is most certain that a Woman's Honour cannot be better entrenched than after this manner, in Circle within Circle, amidst such a Variety of Outworks and Lines of Circumvallation. A Female who is thus invested in Whale-Bone is sufficiently secured against the Approaches of an ill-bred Fellow, who might as well think of Sir George Etheridge's way of making Love in a Tub, as in the midst of so many Hoops. . . .

The first time I saw a Lady dressed in one of these Petticoats I could not forbear blaming her in my own Thoughts for walking abroad when she was so "near her Time", but soon recovered myself out of my Error, when I found all the Modish Party of the Sex as "far gone" as herself. It is generally thought some crafty Women have thus betrayed their Companions into Hoops, that they might make them accessary to their own Concealments, and by that means escape the Censure of the World; as wary Generals have sometimes dressed two or three dozen of their Friends in their own Habit, that they might not draw upon themselves any particular Attacks from the Enemy. The strutting Petticoat smooths all Distinctions, levels the Mother with the Daughter, and sets Maids and Matrons, Wives and Widows, upon the same bottom. In the meanwhile, I cannot but be troubled to see so many well shaped innocent Virgins bloated up, and waddling up and down like big-bellied Women.

Should this Fashion get among the ordinary People, our publick Ways would be so crowded that we should want Street-room . . .

Though you have taken a Resolution, in one of your Papers, to avoid descending to Particularities of Dress, I believe you will not think it below you, on so extraordinary an Occasion, to Unhoop the fair Sex, and cure this fashionable Tympany that is got among them. I am apt to think the Petticoat will shrink of its own Accord at your first coming to Town; at least a Touch of your Pen will make it contract itself, like the Sensitive Plant, and by that means oblige several who are either terrifyed or astonished at this portentous Novelty, and among the rest, Your Humble Servant . . .

The Spectator

1711

I must not here omit an Adventure which happened to us in a Country Church upon the Frontiers of Cornwall. As we were in the midst of the Service, a Lady who is the chief Woman of the Place and had passed the Winter at London with her Husband, entered the Congregation in a little Head-dress and a Hoop'd-Petticoat. The People, who were wonderfully startled at such a sight, all of them rose up. Some stared at the prodigious Bottom, and some at the little Top of this strange Dress. In the mean time the Lady of the Mannor filled the Area of the Church, and walked up to her Pew with an unspeakable Satisfaction, amidst the Whispers, Conjectures and Astonishments of the whole Congregation.

The Spectator

1711

The Farthingale Reviewed, or, More Work for the Cooper.

> I own the female world is much estranged
> From what it was, and top and bottom changed:
> The head was once their darling constant care,
> But women's heads can't heavy burdens bear—
> As much, I mean, as they can do elsewhere;
> So wisely they transferred the mode of dress,
> And furnished t'other end with the excess.
> What tho' like spires or pyramids they show,
> Sharp at the top, and vast of bulk below?
> It is a sign they stand the more secure:
> A maypole will not like a church endure,
> And ships at sea, when stormy winds prevail,
> Are safer in their ballast than their sail.
>
> Hail, happy coat! for modern damsels fit,
> Product of ladies' and of taylors' wit;
> Child of Invention rather than of Pride,
> What Wonders dost thou show, what wonders hide.
> Within the shelter of thy useful shade,
> Thin Galatea's shrivelled limbs appear
> As plump and charming as they did last year;
> Whilst tall Miranda her lank shape improves,
> And graced by thee, in some proportion moves
> Ev'n those who are diminutively short
> May please themselves and make their neighbours sport,
> When to their armpits harnessed up in thee,
> Nothing but head and petticoats we see.
> But oh! what a figure fat Sempronia makes!
> At her gigantick form the pavement quakes;
> By thy addition she's so much enlarged,
> Where'er she comes, the sextons now are charged
> That all church doors and pews be wider made—
> A vast advantage to a joiner's trade.

Quoted in *The Corset and the Crinoline*

1713

Mr. Guardian,

Your predecessor, the "Spectator" endeavoured, but in vain, to improve the charms of the fair sex by exposing their dress whenever it launched into extremities. Amongst the rest the great petticoat came under his consideration, but in contradiction to whatever he has said, they still resolutely persist in this fashion. The form of their bottom is not, I confess altogether the same, for whereas before it was one of an orbicular make, they now look as if they were pressed so that they seem to deny access to any part but the middle. Many are the inconveniences that accrue to her majesty's loving subjects from the said petticoats, as hurting men's shins, sweeping down the ware of industrious females in the street, etc. . . . I saw a young lady fall down the other day, and believe me, sir, she very much resembled an over-turned bell without a clapper. Many other disasters I could tell you of that befall themselves as well as others by means of this unwieldy garment. I wish, Mr. Guardian, you would join with me in showing your dislike of such a monstrous fashion, and I hope, when the ladies see this, the opinion of two of the wisest men in England, they will be convinced of their folly. I am, sir, your daily reader. . . .

The Guardian

1716

Vienna—I will keep my promise in giving you an account of my first going to Court.

In order to that ceremony, I was squeezed up in a gown, and adorned with a gorget and the other implements thereunto belonging: a dress very inconvenient, but which certainly shews the neck and shape to great advantage. I cannot forbear in this place giving you some description of the fashions here, which are more monstrous and contrary to all common sense and reason, than 'tis possible for you to imagine. . . . Their whalebone petticoats outdo ours by several yards' circumference, and cover some acres of ground.

1717

Adrianople—I went to the bagnio about ten o'clock. I was in my travelling habit, which is a riding dress, and certainly appeared very extraordinary to them. . . . The lady that seemed the most considerable among them, entreated me to sit by her, and would fain have undressed me for the bath. I excused myself with some difficulty. They being all so earnest in persuading me, I was at last forced to open my shirt, and shew them my stays; which satisfied them very well, for, I saw, they believed I was so locked up in that machine, that it was not in my own power to open it, which contrivance they attributed to my husband.

LADY MARY WORTLEY MONTAGU, *Letters*

1717

I believe it would puzzle the quickest invention to find out one tolerable convenience in these machines. I appeal to the sincerity of the ladies, whether they are not a great incumbrance upon all occasions (vanity apart) both at home and abroad. What skill and management is required to reduce one of these circles within the limits of a chair, or to find space for two in a chariot; and what precautions must a modest female take even to enter at the doors of a private family without obstruction; Then a vivacious damsel cannot turn herself round in a room a little inconsiderately without oversetting everything like a whirlwind: stands and tea-tables, flower-pots, China-jars and basins innumerable, perish daily by this spreading mischief, which, like a Comet, spares nothing that comes within its sweep. Neither is this fashion more ornamental than convenient. Nothing can be imagined more unnatural, and consequently less agreeable. When a slender Virgin stands upon a basis so exorbitantly wide, she resembles a funnel, a figure of no great elegancy; and I have seen many fine ladies of a low stature, who, when they sail in their hoops about an appartment, look like children in Go-carts.

Weekly Journal

1724   *Les Paniers ou les Vieilles Précieuses*

ARLEQUIN: "J'ai," dit-il, "des bannes, des cerceaux, des paniers, des vollans, des criardes, des matelas piqués et des sacrifices. J'en ai de 'solides', qui ne peuvent lever, à l'usage des prudes; des 'plians' pour les galantes, et des 'mixtes' pour les dames du tiers état. Sçavez-vous, que j'ay quinze ouvrières employées depuis quinze jours à faire un panier en cullote pour la femme d'un procurieur. J'en ai de toute espèce, à l'angloise, à la françoise, à l'espagnole, à l'italienne. J'en fais en cerceaux de porteurs d'eau pour les tailles rondelettes, en 'bannes' pour les minces, en 'lanternes' pour les Venus sans 'matelas postèrieurs'.

Quoted by A. DE LA FIZELIÈRE, *L'Histoire de la Crinoline au temps passé*

c. 1728

On ne croiroit jamais que le cardinal de Noailles a été embarassé par rapport aux paniers que les femmes portent sous leurs jupes pour les rendre larges et évasées. Ils sont si amples qu'en s'asseyant cela pousse les baleines et fait un écart étonnant, en sorte qu'on a été obligé de faire des fauteuils exprès. Il ne peut pas tenir plus de trois femmes dans de grandes loges de spectacle. Cette mode est devenue extravagante comme tout ce qui est extrême; de manière que les princesses étant assises à côté de la reine, leurs jupes, qui remontoient cachoient celles de Sa Majesté: cela a paru impertinent, mais le remède

25 1719. French fashions became stylised during the last years of Louis XIV. Innovations came from England, where the hoop petticoat was already well established when this caricature of the French version, the "panier", appeared

From a contemporary French caricature, "Marché aux Paniers"

27 **c. 1700.** "A Tailor's Shop", from *Curioser Spiegel*. Men should never deride a woman's changing shape, because the highest grade corsets have always been fashioned by men

26 **c. 1747.** "I then ordered the Vest to be drawn up by a Pully to the Top of my great Hall, and afterwards to be spread open in such a Manner that it formed a very splendid and ample Canopy over our Heads."

The *Tatler*, January 4th, 1710

étoit difficile et, à force d'y rêver, le cardinal a trouvé qu'il y auroit toujours un fauteuil vide de chaque côté de la reine, ce qui l'empêcheroit d'être incommodée.

E. J. F. BARBIER, Journal

1729

Les dames n'en veulent pas démordre. Les paniers, plus grands qu'ils n'ont encore été, quoiqu'aussi embarassants pour celles qui les portent qu'incommodes et choquants pour les autres, sont toujours fort à leur gré. Elles les chérissent extrêment, et il n'y a pas jusqu'aux servantes qui ne sauraient aller au marché sans paniers. On prétend que cette mode outrée et hors de toute raison est né en Allemagne, d'où elle passa en Angleterre, et que les dames anglaises ont porté l'ampleur des paniers au point où nous les voyons aujourd'hui. Ils sont plus de trois aunes de tour. On les fait tenir en état par le moyen de petites bandes de nattes faîtes de jonc ou de petites lames d'acier, mais plus ordinairement avec de la baleine qui est fort flexible, qui se casse moins et qui rend les paniers moins pesants. Ceux qu'on appelle "à coudes" sont plus commodes que ceux "à gueridon". Ils forment mieux l'ovale que les autres. Les paniers ont ordinairement cinq rangs de cercles. Ceux "à l'anglaise" en ont huit et sont beaucoup plus chers. Les prix en toile glacée ou en taffetas sont de dix à cinquante livres. Ceux qui sont tressés de galons d'or et d'argent et de broderie se paient en conséquence. <i>Le Mercure</i>

1731

The Stay is a part of modern dress that I have an invincible aversion to, as giving a stiffness to the whole frame, which is void of all grace, and an enemy of beauty; but, as I would not offend the ladies by absolutely condemning what they are fond of I will recall my censure, and only observe that even this female is changing mode continually, and favours or distresses the enemy according to the humour of the wearer. Sometimes, the Stomacher almost rises to the chin, and a modesty-bit serves the purpose of a Ruff; at other times it is so complaisant as not to reach half way, and the modesty is but a transparent shade to the beauties underneath. This is what one may call opening the windows of Heaven, and giving us a view of Paradise; the other shuts up every avenue, and makes Reserve a Dragon for its security, the first may give passion too great a licence, and the last may be an injury to nature; Coquets are the encouragers of one, and Prudes of the other. <i>Weekly Register</i>

1733

The Royal Wedding—The Princess of Orange's dress was the prettiest thing that ever was seen—a "corps de robe", that is, in plain English, a stiff-bodied gown. The eight peers' daughters that held up her train were in the same sort of dress—all white and silver, with great quantities of jewels in their hair, and long locks: some of them were very pretty and well-shaped—it is a most becoming dress.

1738

Yesterday I bespoke a hoop petticoat, of the exact dimensions of my old one; the fashionable hoops are made of the richest damask, trimmed with gold and silver, fourteen guineas a hoop. Would you have me bespeak you such a one against you come?

1743

My new maid promises very well, and she has a sprightliness without pertness that pleases very well, and wears no hoop.

1744

Ireland—I am very sorry to find here and everywhere people out of character . . . but the dairymaids wear large hoops and velvet hoods instead of the round light petticoat and straw hat.

1746

There is such a variety in the manner of dress, that I don't know what to tell you is the fashion; the only thing that seems general are hoops of an enormous size, and most people wear vast winkers to their heads.

1750

I am glad you detest the tubs of hoops—I keep within bounds, endeavouring to avoid all particularities of being too much in or out of fashion.

1754

Yesterday after chapel the Duchess brought home Lady Coventry to feast me, and a feast she was ... her dress was a black silk sack, made for a large hoop, which she wore without any, and it trailed a yard on the ground.

1755

Hoops only worn when full dressed, and those large.

1773

As to the darling's stays, it may be time eno' when you and I have a conference about them; but if a good air is not settled from the beginning, it is as difficult to be attained afterwards as good manners if neglected. (great-niece, born 1771.)

1775

I hope Miss Sparrow will not fall into the absurd fashion of ye wasp-waisted ladies. Dr. Pringle declares he has had four of his patients martyrs to that folly (indeed wickedness), and when they were open'd it was evident that their deaths were occasioned by strait laceing.

1785

I attended her R.H. for several weeks once when her dresser was ill. A new pair of stays happened to be brought, the Princess told me the Queen would come in to see if they fitted properly. When her Majesty came in she felt them here and there, saying, "Elizabeth, they are too tight." "Indeed, mamma, they are not" was the answer. Then turning to me the Queen said, "What do you think?" I said that her R.H. must be the best judge if they did not hurt her, and thus ended the business.

MRS. DELANY, *Autobiography and Correspondence*

1741   *"The Modern Hoop Petticoat"*

As to the Original of the Hoop, whether it was an Invention, as some say, of our own Country-women, or, as others, that it was first imported from France, I will not venture to determine; for the most learned Connisseurs in female Architecture cannot settle this Point, and I have consulted the Records of "Pauline" and other Habit Shops about Covent Garden, without finding any satisfactory Account. I am apt to imagine, that it took its first Rise only by enlarging the Form of the ancient Fardingale, and was confin'd to a very moderate and decent Circumference; But when Innovations of any kind are introduced, it is very difficult to know to what a Degree they may be carried: This has been the Fate of this very Petticoat, which from its Circumference originally took the Name of a "Hoop"; but which at present extends itself into a wide oblong Form, has nothing of the primitive "Hoop" but its mere Name left. When we consider what Alterations have been made in the lower Part of the Female Dress, and think of the different Figures which our Great Grandmothers made with their Petticoats clinging about their Feet, from the Ladies spreading Coats of this last Age, it admits of a Dispute whether the old Habit was the more modest, or the modern more polite. I have heard it objected, that the ancient Petticoat must necessarily too much confine the Woman's Legs; whereas the circular Hoop gave the Feet a Freedom of Motion, shew'd the Beauty of the Leg and Foot which play beneath it, and gain'd Admirers when the Face was too homely to attract the Heart of any Beholder; Some polite Defenders of the late 'convex cupolo' Hoops have observ'd in their Favour, that they serv'd to keep men at a proper Distance, and a Lady within that Circle, seem'd to govern in a spacious Verge sacred to herself. I will not here give as many Reasons as may be brought to shew the Fallacy of this Argument; be it sufficient, that it was well known that many Ladies, who wore 'hoops' of the greatest Circumference were not of the most impregnable Virtue.

For what Reason I will not pretend to say, but the Ladies have found some Inconvenience surely in the circular "Hoop", that they have chang'd it to that extensive oblong Form they now wear; If that was complain'd of as an Incumbrance, I am certain this must be much more troublesome in the Management both within Doors and without; I have been in a moderate large Room, where there have been but two Ladies, who had not Space enough to move without lifting up their Petticoats higher than their Grandmothers would have thought decent; I believe every one has observed to what Pains a Lady is put, to reduce that wide extended Petticoat to the narrow Limits of a Chair or a Chariot; But let her manage her getting in or out ever so skilfully or modestly, yet, she makes but a very grotesque Figure with her Petticoats standing up half way the Glasses, and her Head just peeping out above them. However, as by Women of Quality some greater Liberties will be taken than is any Way consistent for private Persons to attempt, I would desire my fair Country women, who have no Chairs or Chariots, to reduce the exhorbitant Extent of their Petticoat when they walk in publick Places: But it were to be wish'd, that the Sex in general would introduce a more reasonable Fashion for Coats, and confine them within the Bounds of Decency and Moderation. I know no other Argument should sooner prevail with them, than to acquaint them it is a Mode very disagreeable to the Men in general, as it is in particular to

Your Humble Servant . . .

London Magazine

1751

Hear, ye fair mothers of our Isle,
Nor scorn your poet's homely style.
You think it of importance great
T'ensure your daughters growing straight;
For this, such anxious moments feel,
And ask the friendly aid of steel;
For this import the distant cane,
Or slay the monarch of the main
Your cares of body are confined,
Few fear obliquity of mind;—
Deformity of heart I call
The worst deformity of all.

NATHANIEL COTTON, *Visions in Verse*

1753

"The Beau's Receipt for a Lady's Dress"

Let your gown be a sacque, blew, yellow, or green,
And frizzle your elbows with ruffles sixteen;
Furl off your lawn apron, with flounces in rows,
Puff, and pucker up knots on your arms and your toes;
Make your petticoats short, that a hoop eight yards wide
May decently show how your garters are ty'd

. . .

Throw modesty out from your manners and face;
A-la-mode de François, you're a bit for his Grace.

Salisbury Journal

Middle of Eighteenth Century

The Female Fancy's Garland

You beautiful ladys, that follow the mode,
Where ever you live, or take up your abode,
Pray what is the reason you wear such a load
As hoop'd petticoats, monstrous petticoats, bouncing
hoop'd petticoats, maids?

61

Black patches, and towers of powdered hair,
Which long time you have been accustom'd to wear,
I think on my conscience could never compare
With hoop'd petticoats, monstrous petticoats, bouncing
      hoop'd petticoats, maids.

So strange and fantastick young ladys are grown,
Not only miss Madam, but Gillian and Joan,
They must have such petticoats never was known;
Large hoop'd petticoats, monstrous petticoats, bouncing
      hoop'd petticoats, maids.

When ever they walk thro' the streets or the fields,
Supported along by a light pair of heels,
Their coats takes the compass of coach or cart-wheels;
Large hoop'd petticoats, monstrous petticoats, bouncing
      hoop'd petticoats, maids.

I cannot compare this new mode of the town,
To nothing more like, tho' I know they will frown,
Than to a large hog-tub, that's turn'd up-side down;
Large hoop'd petticoats, monstrous petticoats, bouncing
      hoop'd petticoats, maids.

When ever they pass through the midst of a throng,
The people cries out, least they suffer much wrong,
Make room for the madams now trudging along,
With hoop'd petticoats, monstrous petticoats, bouncing
      hoop'd petticoats, maids.

Now some of the vulgar are apt to reproach
Those ladies, tho' young, and as sound as a roach,
With wonder, how they can crowd into a coach,
With hoop'd petticoats, monstrous petticoats, bouncing
      hoop'd petticoats, maids.

These were not found out in our forefathers days,
But finding them useful in sundry ways,
Pray let us all sing in the petticoats praise,
Large hoop'd petticoats, delicate petticoats, bouncing
      hoop'd petticoats, maids!
      Quoted by F. W. FAIRHOLT, *Satirical Songs and Poems on Costume*

1754

The hoop has lost much of its credit with the female world, and has suffered greatly from the introduction of sacks and negligées. Men will agree that next to no clothing, there is nothing more ravishing than an easy dishabille. Our ladies, for that reason perhaps, come into public places as though they were just out of bed.

      The Connoisseur

1759

Le sieur Panard, tailleur pour dames, invita "La Feuille nécessaire", journal d'annonces, à dire que "tout en continuant à faire des robes de dix façons différentes il étoit inventeur d'un procédé nomme les "Considérations", pour soutenir les robes avec grâce, sans paniers et sans être obligée de porter beaucoup de joupons.

      Quoted by A. DE LA FIZELIÈRE, *L'Histoire de la Crinoline au temps passé*

28 1748.

"Ladies for you this ample Scene I vend,
A new Invention by your Sexes Friend,
With which you may securely trip along
Each narrow Lane, or shun the rustic Throng."

The figure on extreme left shows how a panier should be managed in order to go through
doors, enter a sedan chair, etc.

From a contemporary engraving

29 **1770–1780.** "Tight Lacing; or, Fashion before Ease"

From an engraving after John Collet

30 **c. 1770.** "Sa Taille est ravissante", by Lebeau, after Baudouin. The rigid whaleboned stays, seen here, were worn until nearly the end of the eighteenth century

31 **1750–1755.** Nymphenburg porcelain figure. The lady raises her dress to show her richly decorated panier, whose rows of whalebone, or cane, are clearly seen

The British Museum

1761

If anything should put off your coming (which I hope it won't) pray send a pair of stays for a measure, as the embroidery is to be measured upon them and that is the longest piece of work.

1764

There is nobody but Ly Tavistock, who does not dress French, who is at all genteel, for if they are not French they are so very ill dressed, it's terrible. Almost everybody powders now, and wears a little hoop ... stays very high and pretty tight at bottom ... waist very long.

LADY SARAH LENNOX, *Life and Letters*

1762

Beauty and Fashion

Then of late, you're so fickle that few people mind you;
For my part, I can never tell where to find you;
Now drest in a cap, now naked in none,
Now loose in a mob, now close in a Joan;
Without handkerchief now, and now buried in ruff,
Now plain as a Quaker, now all of a puff;
Now a shape in neat stays, now a slattern in jumps,
Now high in French heels, now low in your pumps;
Now monstr'ous in hoop, now trapish, and walking
With your petticoats clung to your heels, like a maulkin;
Like the cock on the tower, that shews you the weather,
You are hardly the same for two days together.

London Magazine

1770's

Tous les soirs à six heures Mesdames interrompaient la lecture que je leur faisais, pour se rendre avec les princes chez Louis XV: cette visite s'appelait "le débotter du roi", et était accompagnée d'une sorte d'étiquette. Les princesses passaient un énorme panier, qui soutenait une jupe chamarée d'or ou de broderie; elles attachaient autour de leur taille une longue queue, et cachaient le négligé du reste de leur habillement par un grand mantelet de taffetas noir, qui les enveloppait jusque sous le menton ... Le roi baisait chaque princesse au front, et la visite était si courte, que la lecture, interrompue par cette visite, recommencait souvent au bout d'un quart d'heure; Mesdames rentraient chez elles, dénouaient les cordons de leur jupe et de leur queue, reprenaient leur tapisserie, et moi mon livre.

MME CAMPAN, *Mémoires sur la Vie de Marie Antoinette*

1762

It will be warmer, I hope, by the King's Birthday, or the old ladies will catch their deaths. There is a court dress to be instituted—(to thin the Drawing-rooms)—stiff-bodied gowns and bare shoulders. What dreadful discoveries will be made both on fat and lean! I recommend to you the idea of Mrs. Cavendish, when half-stark; and I might fill the rest of my paper with such images, but your imagination will supply them.

1777

There has been a young gentlewoman overturned and terribly bruised by her Vulcanian stays. They now wear a steel busk down their middle, and a rail of the same metal across their breasts. If a hero attempts to storm such strong lines, and comes to a close engagement, he must lie as ill at ease as St. Lawrence on his gridiron (32).

1783

On pretend that certain invisible machines, of which one heard much a year or two ago, and which were said to be constructed of cork, and to be worn somewhere or other behind, are now to be transplanted somewhere before, in imitation of the Duchess of Devonshire's pregnancy.

HORACE WALPOLE, *Letters*

1770

Prologue to the "Spanish Barber"

This summer—for I love a little prance—
This summer, gentlefolks, I've been to France:
. . . .
France charms our ladies, naked bards and beaux
Who smuggle there their learning and their cloaths
Buckles like grid-irons, and wigs on springs;
"Têtes" built like towers, and rumps like ostrich wings.
If this piece please, each summer I'll go over,
And fetch new patterns by the Straits of Dover.

London Magazine

32   Bath stays or the lady's steel shapes

1777

    To be serious; that a cut of a coat, a size of a buckle, the length of streamers, or the largeness of hips, should be deemed capable of contributing to happiness, is more than ridiculous. It is preposterous madness. What species of felicity can a lover expect in a "cork rump"? The most antiquated virgin, in the list of grizzly prudes, would be far more acceptable than a blooming beauty, with such pieces of levity behind her.

London Magazine

1777

Let her gown be tuck'd up to the hips on each side
Shoes too high for to walk or to jump;
And to deck the sweet creature complete for a bride
Let the cork-cutter cut her a rump.

66

Thus finish'd in taste, while on Chloe you gaze,
You may take the dear charmer for life;
But never undress her—for, out of her stays,
You'll find you have lost half your wife.

London Magazine

"Paltry Pride"

There's the ladies of fashion you see,
    They'll all have a turn at this pride,
They must have cork rumps, I declare,
    And a head as big as a bee-hive,
With a great tod of wool on each hip,
    To make them look much in the fashion,
And a bag hanging down to their waist,
    I think the devil ought to fetch them.
Quoted by F. W. FAIRHOLT, *Satirical Songs and Poems on Costume*

1775

Stays quite low before, and the bosom much exposed. Undress—all sorts of worked gowns over small hoops.

1776

Full dress—Stays exceedingly low, large hoops.

1780

Full dress—Shapes small, long waists, festino gowns over large hoops.

Lady's Magazine

c. **1777**

Culs postiches—Madame de Matignon, arrivant de Naples, fut obligée d'aller sur-le-champ à Marly, où étoit la cour; elle ne s'arrêta à Paris que pour y coucher; elle n'y avoit vu que deux ou trois personnages très-graves, qui n'avoient pas imaginé de la mettre au fait des modes nouvelles: il s'en étoit établi une, devenue universalle depuis douze ou quinze jours. Cette mode, qui n'avoit rapport qu'à l'habillement des femmes, consistoit à se mettre par-derrière, au bas de la taille, et sur la croupe, un paquet plus ou moins gros, plus ou moins parfait de ressemblance, auquel on donnoit sans détour le nom de 'cul'. Madame de Matignon ignoroit complètement l'établissement de cette singulière mode. Elle n'arriva à Marly que pour se coucher; on la logea dans un appartement qui n'étoit separé de celui qu'occupoit Madame de Rully que par un cloison très-mince et une porte condamnée; qu'on se figure, s'il est possible, la surprise de Madame de Matignon, lorsque le lendemain, deux heures après son reveil, elle entendit entrer chez madame de Rully madame la princesse d'Hénin, qu'elle reconnut à la voix, et qui, sur-le-champ, dit: "Bonjour, mon cœur; montrez-moi votre 'cul' ..." Madame de Matignon, petrifiée, écouta attentivement, et recueillit le dialogue suivant. Madame d'Hénin, reprenant la parole, s'écria, avec le ton de l'indignation: "Mais, mon cœur, il est affreux, votre 'cul'; étroit, mesquin, tombant; il est affreux, vous dis-je. En voulez-vous voir un joli? tenez, regardez le mien ..." "Ah! c'est vrai!" reprit madame de Rully, avec l'accent de l'admiration. "Regardez donc, mademoiselle Aubert (c'étoit sa femme de chambre, présente à cette scène); il est rebondi! ... le mien est si plat, si maigre! ... Ah! le joli, le joli 'cul'." "Voilà, comme il faut avoir un 'cul'; quand on veut réussir dans le monde. Il est bien heureux que j'aie été chargée du soin de vous surveiller."

c. **1770**

Présentation à Versailles.—Mesdames de Puisieux et d'Estrée me persécutèrent véritablement le lendemain, jour de ma présentation ... elles voulurent que j'eusse mon "grand corps" pour dîner, afin, disoient-elles, de m'y accoutumer: ces grands corps laissoient les épaules découvertes, coupoient les bras et gênoient horriblement: d'ailleurs, pour montrer ma taille, elles me firent serrer à l'outrance.

... On me fit grâce du grand panier pour le dîner, quoiqu'il fut question un moment de me le faire prendre pour m'y accoutumer aussi ... tout le dîner se passa en discussions sur ma toilette. Je ne mangeai rien du tout, parce que j'étois si serrée que je pouvois à peine respirer.

BALS PARÉS. On appeloit "bals parés", dans le dernier siècle, ceux qui se donnoient à la cour dans les occasions solenelles ... Les dames de la cour n'y dansoient qu'en grands habits, avec d'énormes paniers : des grands corps dont les épaulettes découvrant les épaules, permettoient à peine de lever les bras ; des chaussures étroites et pointues, portées sur de hauts talons ; des bas de robes d'une longueur immenses ; un habit d'une épaisse et riche étoffe brodée d'or ; une coiffure d'une prodigieuse élévation et surchargée de pierreries ; de lourdes girandoles de diamans suspendus aux oreilles complétoient ce costume, avec lequel il étoit difficile de danser lestement.

CORPS BALEINÉS. On a beaucoup declamé contres les corps, qui sont en effet très dangereux lorsqu'ils sont trop étroits ; mais quand ils ne gênoient pas, ils élargissoient prodigieusement la poitrine en jetant les épaules en arrière. On a remarqué que, depuis qu'on n'en porte plus, les maladies de poitrine sont infiniment plus communes parmi les femmes. Enfin les corps baleinés avoient un grand avantage, celui de préserver les enfans du danger de presque toutes les chutes.

PARURE. Le costume de femmes du dix-huitième siècle étoit fort ridicule ; mais les femmes étoient beaucoup plus parées qu'elles ne peuvent l'être aujourd'hui ; car la grande parure, grâce aux grands paniers, avoit un étalage éblouissant. Il est impossible de se faire une idée de l'éclat d'un cercle composé d'une trentaine de femmes bien parées, assises à côté les unes des autres. Leurs énormes paniers formoient un riche espalier, artistement couvert de fleurs ; de perles, d'argent, d'or, de paillons de couleur et de pierreries. L'effet de toutes ces brillantes parures réunies ne peut se décrire. ... Mais les femmes de ce temps, qui avoient un tel goût, étoient d'autant plus inexcusables, que la parure alors étoit un vrai supplice. Il falloit subir l'opération de deux mille papillons sur la tête, d'une coiffure qui duroit deux heures, et dont l'extrême élévation étoit aussi incommodé que ridicule. Il falloit se serrer à l'outrance dans un corps baleiné, s'affubler d'un panier de trois aunes, et marcher sur des espèces d'échasses ; on peut plaire aujourd'hui avec moins de frais, et surtout moins de peine.

MME DE GENLIS, *Mémoires depuis 1756 jusqu'à nos Jours*

c. 1780

Présentation à la cour.—On ne saurait rien imaginer de plus ridicule que cette répétition de la présentation. M. Huart (mon maître à danser), gros homme, coiffé admirablement et poudré à blanc, avec un jupon bouffant, représentait la reine et se tenait debout au fond du salon. Il me dictait ce que je devais faire, tantôt personnifiant la dame qui me présentait, tantôt retournant à la place de la reine pour figurer le moment où, ôtant mon gant et m'inclinant pour baiser le bas de sa robe elle faisait le mouvement de m'en empêcher. Rien n'était oublié ou negligé dans cette répétition qui se renouvela pendant trois ou quatre heures de suite. J'avais un grand habit, le grand panier, le bas et le haut du corps vêtus d'une robe du matin, et les cheveux simplement relevés. C'était une veritable comédie. Le dimanche matin, après la messe, ma présentation eut lieu. J'étais en grand corps, c'est-à-dire avec un corset fait exprès, sans épaulettes, lacé par derrière, la gorge entièrement découverte. Sept ou huit rangs de gros diamants que la reine avait voulu me prêter cachaient en partie la mienne. Le devant du corset était comme lacé par des rangs de diamants. J'en avais encore sur la tête une quantité, soit en épis, soit en aigrettes.

MARQUISE DE LA TOUR DU PIN, *Journal d'une Femme de Cinquante Ans*

1778

My dear Louisa, you will laugh when I tell you, that poor Winifred, who was reduced to be my gentlewoman's gentlewoman, broke two laces in endeavouring to draw my new French stays close. You know I am naturally small at bottom but now you might literally span me. You never saw such a doll. Then, they are so intolerably wide across the breast, that my arms are absolutely sore with them ; and my sides so pinched!—But it is the 'ton' ; and pride feels no pain. It is with these sentiments the ladies of the present age heal their wounds ; to be admired, is a sufficient balsam.

GEORGIANA CAVENDISH, DUCHESS OF DEVONSHIRE, *The Sylph*

Se vend a Augsbourg dans le Negoce commun de l'Academie Imperiale d'Empire sous son Privilege et avec defense de n'enfaire ni vendre de Cop.

33 **c. 1775.** "The Old Coquette." She is wearing whaleboned stays, lacing in front, and two separate side hoops, or paniers, as worn for "undress"

From a contemporary German caricature

34 **1785.** "The Bum Shop", by Thomas Rowlandson. False "bums", "rumps", or "culs postiches" appeared during the last quarter of the eighteenth century. The next century, whose nomenclature was less robust, called them "bustles"

From a contemporary print

1780

The perfection of figure according to the then fashion was the smallness of the circumference into which your unfortunate waist could be compressed, and many a poor girl hurt her health very materially by trying to rival the reigning beauty of that day, the Duchess of Rutland, who was said to squeeze herself to the size of an orange and a half. Small hoops were worn in a morning and larger for a dress, some going outwards as they went downwards, something in the form of a bell; sacques were very common; my mother constantly wore them. They were dresses with loose backs and a stomacher.

MARY FRAMPTON, *Journal*

1782

The favour, dear Madam, we wish of you, is to remonstrate with these smart gentlemen, and with us, tell them they are incapable of correcting the foibles in the ladies' dresses till they have established a criterion of their own . . . till then we must insist that the hoop (the battery at which most of their present artillery is played off against), when of a moderate size, is an addition to the appearance of a fine woman; it is a finishing grace to their persons, and gives them that dignity of appearance that every woman in a genteel line of life has a right to assume. *Lady's Magazine*

1789

Changes in French Fashions.—The advantages of a good shape are often injured by the foolish fondness of having them very slender. Were they to consult the form of the superb antique statue of Venus, they would find a good proportion as far removed from a too slender waist, and uniform, as a clumsy one. Besides, it may be justly observed, that when the corsets are too closely laced, it takes away entirely all ease and grace. The motion becomes stiff, and the attitude constrained; without speaking of the accidents which may result from such an outrage against Nature. A great vulgarism in taste much prevailed some years ago—Women who were very lusty were anxious to excel in the art of puffing, which had been ingeniously imagined by those of a slender make to supply what Nature had refused them.—You might then have seen very little women, who, by adopting this ridiculous mode, might be really said to have more breadth than length. *Lady's Monthly Museum*

c. 1792–3

The first reformation made in my appearance was effected by a stay-maker. I was stood on the window-seat, whilst a man measured me for the machine, which, in consideration of my youth, was to be only what was called half-boned, that is, instead of having the bones placed as close as they could lie, an interval the breadth of one was left vacant between each. Notwithstanding, the first day of wearing them was very nearly purgatory, and I question if I was sufficiently aware of the advantage of a fine shape to reconcile me to the punishment. ELIZABETH HAM, *Elizabeth Ham by Herself*

1793

The fashion of dressing, at present, is to appear "prominent", and the stays are made accordingly. This is holding out a wish to be thought in a thriving way, even without the authority of the "Arches Court" of Canterbury—something in the French way—a philosophical desire to be "conspicuously great" with MISCHIEF, without any regard to law or reason. The idea was at first sent forward by a few "dropsical" ladies.

1795

Corsettes about six inches long, and a slight buffon tucker of two inches high, are now the only defensive paraphernalia of our fashionable belles, between the necklace and the apron strings.

1799

The fashion of false bosoms has at least this utility, that it compels our fashionable fair to wear something. *The Times*

1790's

The bosom, which Nature planted at the bottom of her chest, is pushed up by means of wadding and whalebone to a station so near her chin that in a very full subject that feature is sometimes lost between the invading mounds. The stays—or coat of mail—must be laced as tight as strength can draw the cord. Not only is the shape thrust out of its proper place but the blood is thrown forcibly into the face, neck and arms ... and were it not for the fine apparel of our ladies we should be at a loss at the first glance to decide, by their redundancy and universal redness, whether they were nurses or cooks. Over this strangely manufactured figure a scanty petticoat and as scanty a gown are put. The latter resembles a bolster-slip rather than a garment (54).   *Morning Herald*

1799

Fashions from Paris.—The female citizen Lesfraud has published a state of the fancy robes, and other articles of fashion recently invented by herself ... She has also designed the handkerchief a la Flore of taffeta, ornamented with ribbands, which serve for a girdle, and also the taffeta corsets to preserve the graceful shape of the person, very lightly whaleboned.   *Lady's Magazine*

35   Shepherds, I have lost my waist! Have you seen my body? (1795)

c. 1794   *"The Short Body'd Gown"*

Ye lads and ye lassies of country and city,
I pray you give ear to my humerous ditty,
Concerning the fashion just come to town,
A whimsical dress call'd the short body'd gown.

This humerous dress that's now call'd the mode,
Surpasses all fashions that e'er was in vogue,
There's not a young miss in the country all round,
But must be stuff'd up in a short body'd gown.
. . .
Both maids, wives, and widows, you'd think were all wild
And all look as if they were got with child,
Neither baloons, nor turbans, or all fashions round,
Will fit them, unless they've a new body'd gown.

      Quoted by F. W. FAIRHOLT, *Satirical Songs and Poems on Costume*

CHAPTER III

Beginning of the Nineteenth Century to 1925

1

THE CORSET

AT the beginning of the nineteenth century the Grecian figure—the natural figure (high rounded breasts, long well-rounded limbs)—was the ideal every woman hoped to attain. Her soft, light muslin dress clung to her body and showed every contour, so all superfluous undergarments which might spoil the silhouette were discarded—among them the boned stay. In France, where the social order had been completely overturned, with consequent loosening of morals and deportment, this fashion was more followed than in England. There are, however, so many references in English and French writings of the time, both to the use and disuse of stays, that it may be presumed that both styles held good, and the young girl, or the woman with a beautiful figure, did indeed discard her stays, but those less fortunately created had to resort to some subterfuge in order to wear the very simple robes and keep their too redundant flesh within fashionable bounds.

Many of the simple muslin dresses of about 1800 are mounted on a cotton lining with two separate side pieces which cross over and fasten in front, under and supporting the breasts, and this acted as a kind of brassière and was often the only form of stays worn. But in many cases this was not enough; in England the whaleboned stays of the late eighteenth century continued to be worn, sometimes to suit the prevailing mode they came right down over the hips, where the earlier tabs were replaced by gussets. For the very thin this garment was reinforced by padding, for the stout it was heavily boned. As this type of long corset is only seen illustrated in caricatures of the period it was probably not fashionable wear but an aid to control an unfashionable figure (101).

Various other experiments seem to have been made to give the true Grecian form, among them a long, knitted corset of silk or cotton. It is significant that in France the old name *corps* had quite disappeared, and from now on any tight-fitting body garment is known as a "corset", a fashion that was copied in England though the old form "stays" was also retained.

In French and English women's journals round about 1809–1810 there was an outcry against the return of the corset: a longer body, fuller skirts, and more emphasised waistline in the dress having brought it back into favour again (54).

A new type of corset began to take shape, completely different from its predecessor the whaleboned stays; this time the emphasis was not on a rigid, straight body but on curved lines flowing out from a small waist. Again it began from a simple body bodice of

75

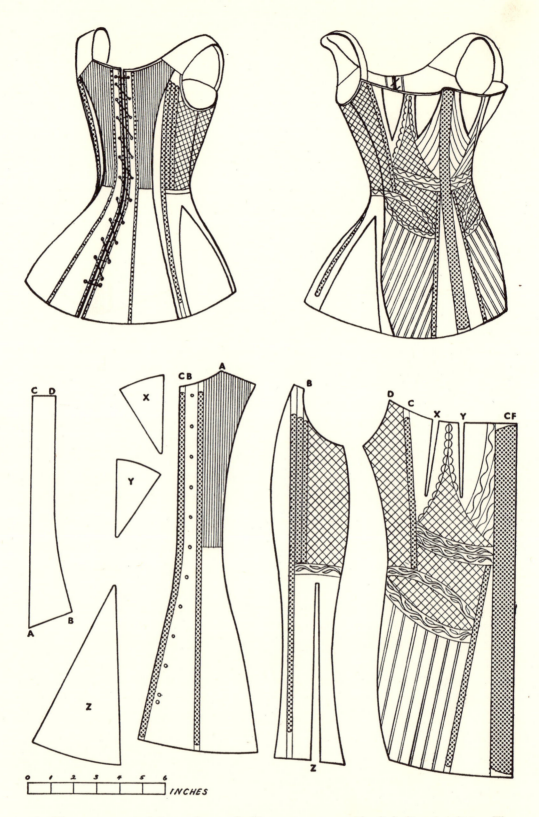

36. These stays are made in two layers of white cotton sateen, with a light linen interlining. They are beautifully quilted round the waist; lightly boned, the centre busk is missing. The eyelet holes are worked (*late 1820's*)

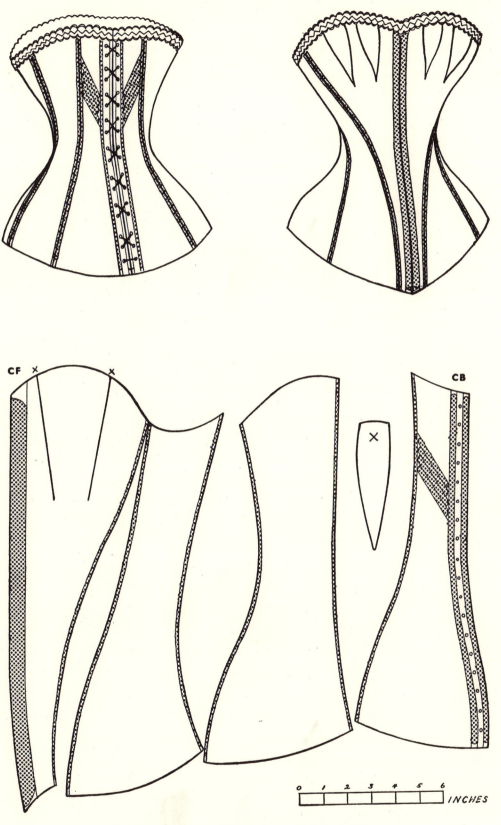

37   Pattern for corset; to be boned on each seam (*1844*)

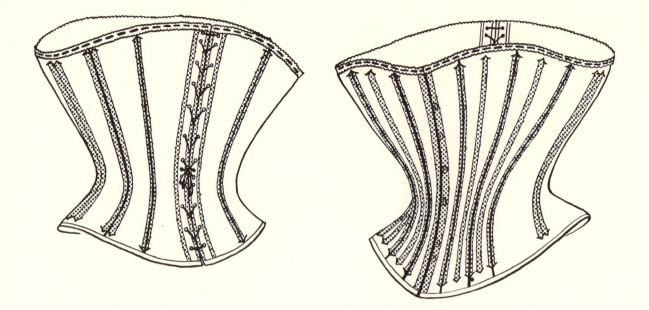

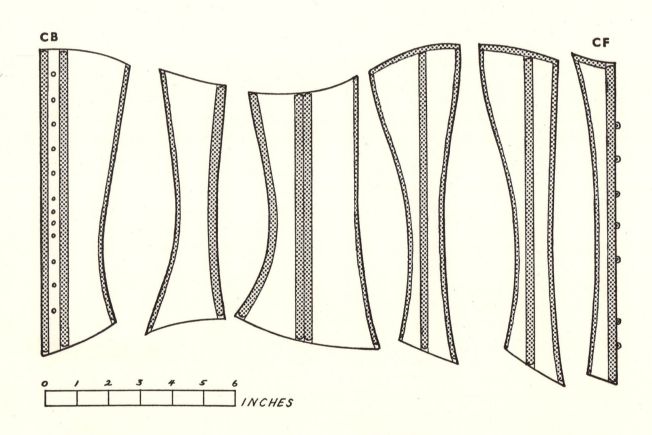

CB

CF

0 1 2 3 4 5 6
INCHES

38　Light French stays in white cotton with small spot flower, trimmed lace, unlined. This way of cutting from shaped
pieces, without gussets, came in in the late 1840's. It was more popular in France than in England (c. *1860*)

strong cotton material (*jean*, later known as *coutil*); while the waist was still high, two pieces for the front and two for the back were sufficient, the centre front seams sometimes and the centre back as a rule being shaped; roundness was given to the bust by inserting two or more gussets on each side of the front at the top of the corset, and one or more gussets on each side at the base to accommodate the hips. As the waist gradually lengthened and became more defined extra side pieces were added (36, 105) or, from about 1835, a basque shaped piece fitting the hips. At first, while the dress was still slender, this bodice was fairly long on the hips, but it decreased in length as the skirt increased in fullness, and by the middle of the century was sometimes very short indeed. A broad busk was inserted up the centre front, and narrow whalebones up the centre back; for heavier figures side bones and extra back bones could be added. It usually laced up the centre back and, until the forties, had shoulder straps. Though there were a number of fashionable dressmakers specialising in making corsets—corsetières—they were often made at home, and patterns and instructions for constructing them are to be found in the ladies' magazines as late as the 1860's. These corsets followed the fashionable silhouette, the body to the waist being cut much longer in the forties (37) and becoming much shorter again in the fifties and sixties.

With the development of industry in the nineteenth century many inventions appeared to help the corsetière, such as: metal eyelets in 1828; the first steel front busk fastening in 1829; and various ideas for lacing and unlacing. In 1832 a Frenchman, Jean Werly, took out a patent for woven corsets; they were made on a loom, the shaping gussets being incorporated in the process of weaving. These corsets, usually of white cotton and very lightly boned, were easy to wear and consequently very popular; they continued to be worn until 1889.

In the late 1840's, in France, where lighter-weight corsets were preferred, a new cut was introduced—a corset without gussets, made from seven to thirteen separate pieces, each one being shaped in to the waist. In the 1860's, when the crinoline was at its widest and the main role of the corset was to make the waist small, this type of corset, exceedingly short, was very popular, though more worn on the Continent than in England (38). Stays of the middle of the nineteenth century were lightly boned but stiffened by cording and sometimes quilting; as they were worn over the petticoats and crinoline the centre front busk and back bones were very much curved in to the waist. White corsets were considered more ladylike, though grey, putty, red and then black ones were found more economical; they were generally made of coutil and always lined in white (56–59).

When in the early 1870's the crinoline was discarded in favour of the bustle, or tournure, and the dress began to mould the figure in front and round the hips, the corset really came into its own; it was no longer possible to do with a home-made article and the corset industry received a tremendous impetus. It was also about this date that the ladies' magazines began to give more details and illustrations of the various parts of dress, and advertisements for corsets, until then rather rare, become increasingly frequent. From them will be seen the great variety of types of corset that now began to appear, all designed to meet the requirements of the new line in the dress, the body of which enveloped the hips, this new "cuirasse" body demanding a corset which indeed became a veritable cuirass. Many are the inventions and contrivances advocated, the great difficulty

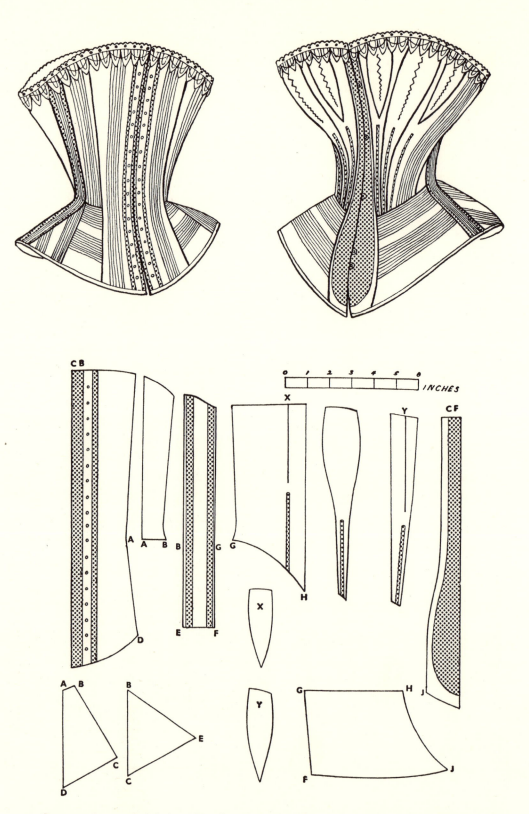

39 Grey coutil corset, lightly boned but heavily corded. The spoon busk and the fact that it is very stiff—steam-moulded—means it must be 1873 or later, but the shape is still that of the 1860's, and the basque very wide (c. 1873)

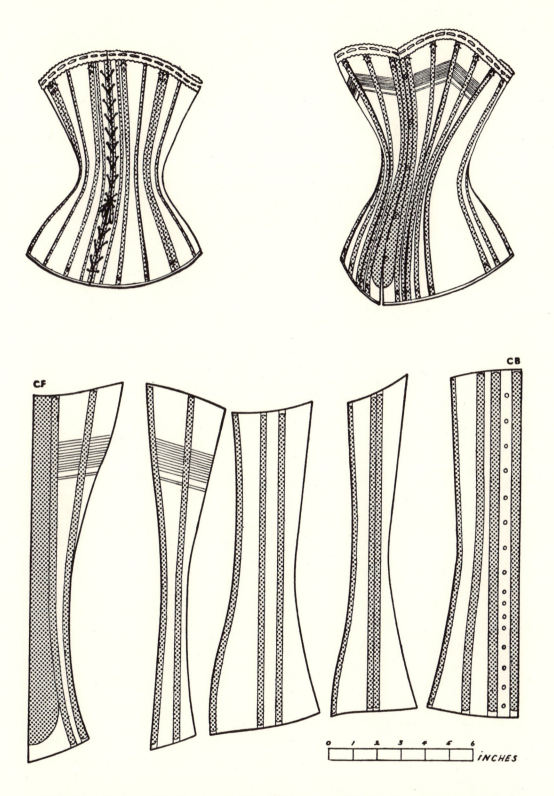

40 Black coutil corset. The bones are held in position top and bottom by yellow arrowheads, the front is reinforced with cords, with yellow stitching between. It is edged with black lace with yellow ribbon. Curved spoon busk (*late 1880's*)

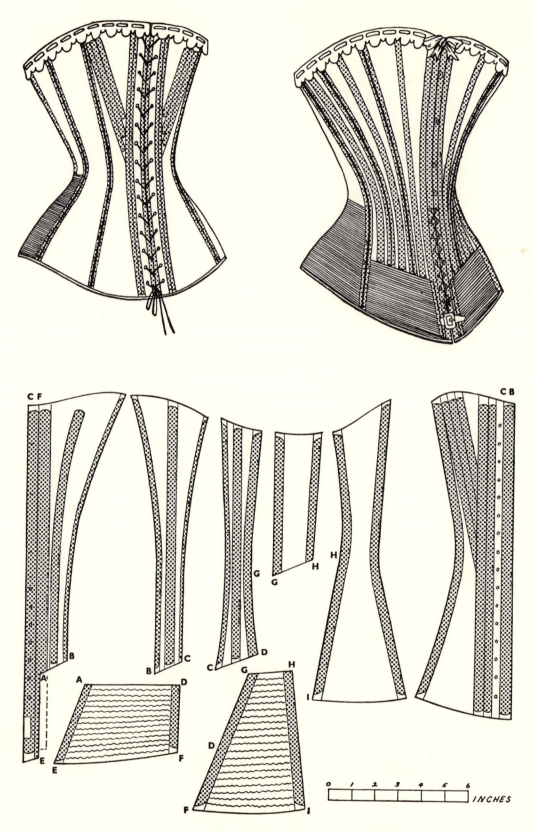

41   Black coutil corset, with elastic insertions (*mid 1890's*)

being to prevent the corset from riding up and wrinkling, and the bones from breaking at the waist—which they frequently did owing to the exaggerated curve of the bust and hips from the incredibly small waist. Various methods of boning were tried out, steel was increasingly used, whalebone was in so much demand that it became scarce and very expensive, and various substitutes, such as cane, had to be used (60, 61).

The two main styles of cutting the corset continued—either with gussets and a basque, or in separate shaped pieces. In the late sixties the process of steam moulding was introduced—the corset when finished was heavily starched and dried to shape on a metal "mannequin" mould. In 1873 a shaped busk—narrow at the top, curving into the waist, and widening out into a pear-shaped base, the "spoon busk" (*busc en poire*)—appeared and was seen on fashionable models until 1889 (42). This steam moulding and spoon busk, as well as more boning and more cording, made the corset a much heavier and more restricting garment (39). One model of the early eighties has twenty shaped pieces and sixteen

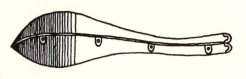

42 "Spoon Busk", 1873

whalebones each side, as well as the spoon busk. Though usually with a front busk fastening, this period occasionally has lacing only, either centre front or centre back, in order to preserve an unbroken line under the smooth tight-fitting corsage of the dress. The corset was worn over the petticoats, which were arranged on a shaped band so as to avoid any unnecessary bulk round the waist; sometimes they were attached to a band fixed to the lower edge of the corset (44). Suspenders only appeared in the late eighties, but until the end of the century were mounted on a separate band tied round the waist; though they solved the problem of keeping the stockings up they created a new one, as the petticoats had now to be worn over the corsets and suspenders and this often interfered with the line of the dress. The corset had now become a very elegant article in a lady's wardrobe and much care was given to its design and execution. There are some lovely specimens of the eighties in black sateen machined with yellow, blue, pink, or green, the bones being held in position by a variety of embroidery stitches: the most expensive might be made of satin, as for example, a white satin wedding corset embroidered with orange blossom. Out-of-date models, usually in grey or putty drill with cording instead of whalebone, continued to be manufactured for the cheaper trade, workhouses, charity institutions, etc.

In the late 1880's the silhouette began to change, it became harder and less rounded and the body longer—what was known as the "Louis XV" line. Rows of cording or short cross strips of whalebone, placed in the top of the corset, sharpened the contours of the bust (40). The centre front steel became narrow again and, though still curved over the abdomen, lost the concave dip into the waist. It was cut on the same principle but more use was made of elastic inserts. The value of elastic in corsetry had long been appreciated, but the quality was still poor and as a corset material it did not really come into its own until the 1920's. The best corsets were of coloured silk, satin, or silk broché, the cheaper ones as usual of grey, putty, or black coutil—they were always lined. The great development of the corset trade began to have results, the improvement in materials and finish meant that the corsetière could now produce an elegant "glove-fitting" garment guaranteed to mould and shape the most difficult figure. This triumph achieved, it is not

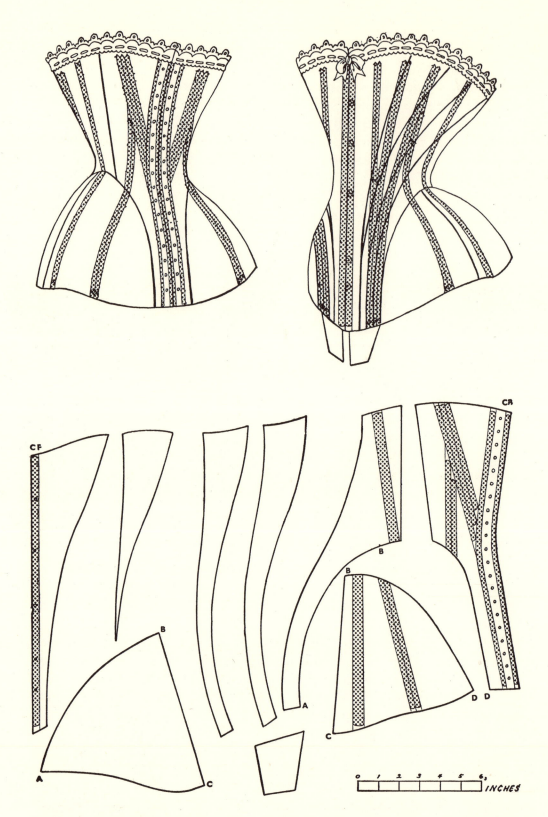

43 Black coutil straight-fronted corset. The complicated boning of the front has not been given in the pattern but can be seen in the sketch of the corset. The two tabs at the bottom of the front busks are for suspenders (*c. 1901*)

surprising that the dressmakers profited and launched out into an entirely new line; skirts began to fit the figure all round, and the hips and behind finally emerged from their centuries-old draperies to become the centre of interest in clothes for a long time to come (41, 62–64, 66).

Throughout the nineteenth century silhouette-emphasis had been on the small waist and curves; the heavier corset of the end of the century exaggerated this still further until the female anatomy was becoming seriously distorted and women's health affected. In 1900 Mme Gaches-Sarraute, of Paris, a corsetière who had studied medicine, designed a new corset to remedy this. Its chief characteristic was the straight-fronted busk, which starting lower on the bust-line continued down over the abdomen without dipping in to the waist, and at the point of the busk, suspenders, now attached to the corset itself, kept

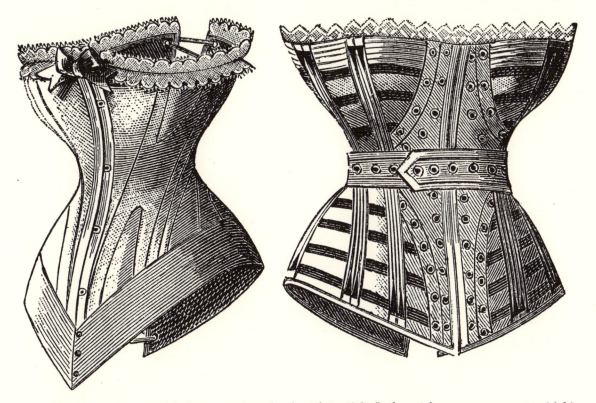

44   The corset silhouette of the late seventies and early eighties (*left*). Light-weight summer corset, *1882* (*right*)

the line taut and unbroken to the knees: it supported the abdomen and left the thorax free. This corset was hailed with delight and immediately adopted by the fashionable woman. Soon, however, exaggeration again crept in, due chiefly to the desire to retain the small waist, and this resulted in the famous "S" curve—the bust billowed out over the low front, and the superfluous abdominal flesh, pressed flat by the heavy front busk, swelled out at the sides on the hips, and on the behind. This corset was a miracle of cutting and shaping; never before or since has it been quite so complicated. It was constructed from numerous curved pieces—as many as ten to fifteen each side, plus gussets—all expertly joined together and traversed by a quantity of whalebone and steel of varying

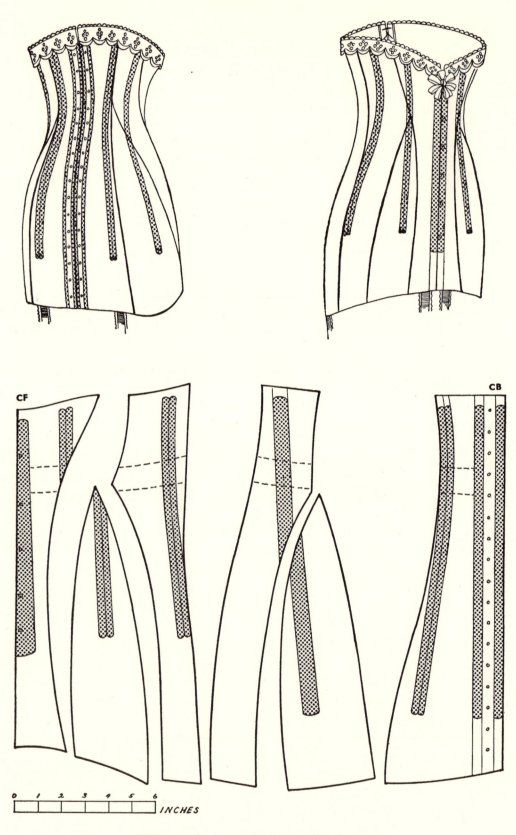

45　White coutil, trimmed broderie anglaise (c. 1911)

degrees of thickness and weight (43). Sometimes these corsets were long, sometimes short, lined or unlined. The expensive ones were of coloured satin, silk or silk broché, trimmed with real lace and ribbon bows; "butterfly" blue was the favourite colour (65, 67, 69).

1904–1905 were the peak years of the "S" curve; from then on the line began slowly to straighten up, though it was not until 1907, when the dresses themselves began to lose their fullness, that the new fashion line, long and svelte, really began to take shape. To help the dressmaker the corsetière, now a past master of his craft, correspondingly obliged by producing a very long straight corset (45), lower still in the bust than the previous mode and fitting well down over the hips. Having a straighter line it was cut from fewer pieces; less boning was used and frequently elastic gussets were inserted at the base for ease of movement. This slender, willowy line came easily to the naturally slim, but for those more encumbered with flesh it could only be attained by sacrificing some more inches at the waist. This style too became exaggerated, the corset being sometimes so long —seventeen inches from the waist—and so tight that hips and sides were rubbed raw, and in some models it was impossible to sit down (71, 74).

Throughout the twentieth century there were attempts to return to an Empire line, and from time to time a leading dressmaker produced a model with a very high waist. But this is a style requiring a slim silhouette and was only really accepted in 1910 when the gown had become sheath-like. The cut of the corset did not alter, but lighter materials and less boning gave suppleness and subtlety to the lines of the figure now more visible under the softer, clinging skirts. The high waist drew attention to the bust and a bust bodice became a necessary supplement to the corset. This Empire line was in full swing when the 1914 War called a halt to further developments.

The bust bodice had appeared about 1900 when the straight-fronted corset came in. Until then, when necessary, shoulder straps on the corset had given the extra support required by a full bust, but with the new low-bust model that was no longer practicable. The corset for the average figure had ceased to have shoulder-straps in the 1840's, though they are seen from the 1890's down to 1914 on models specially designed for wear with tailored suits. The 1900 bust bodice evolved from the earlier "petticoat bodice" of white cotton which was worn in the nineteenth century over the corset to keep it clean and conceal it (cache-corset). Now in 1900 it separated into two distinct garments: made more fitting and lightly boned it was worn by the full-busted woman and became the "bust bodice"; made looser and more decorated it supplied deficiences in the thin woman and became the "camisole". The voluminous underclothes—woollen combinations, over them a heavy, white calico chemise very much trimmed with tucks, insertions of broderie anglaise and lace—were well pulled down inside the corset making a bust bodice unnecessary: but when to accommodate the slimmer line of 1907 underclothes were simplified, and when finally a few years later the Empire waistline was accepted and demanded a higher, more rounded bust, then the bust bodice came into fashion and was more elegantly known by its French name the "brassière" (72, 73).

The war years put a stop to any exaggeration of fashion, but they did bring in looser, more comfortable, hence more shapeless, clothes; the corset too became more comfortable and more shapeless. It must be noted, however, that lighter types of corsets for sports wear, or for wearing with "rest gowns", had already made their appearance in the beginning of the century (46, 68). One model was made of ribbon, another of a knitted weave with

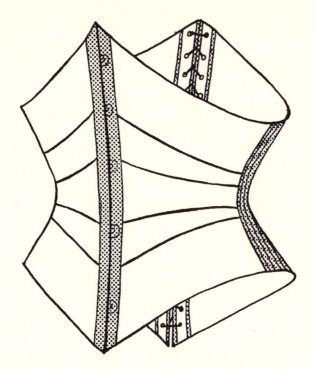

46 This type of light corset was for sport or negligée wear; as they were often made of ribbon they were known as "ribbon corsets". This particular model is made of strips of material—blue sateen coutil and blue broché (c. 1904)

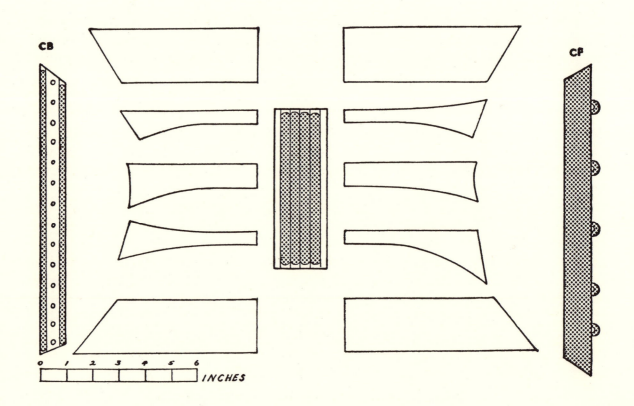

CB

CF

0 1 2 3 4 5 6 *INCHES*

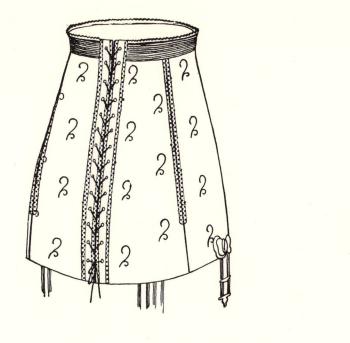
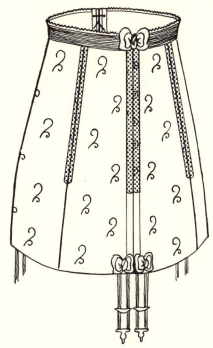

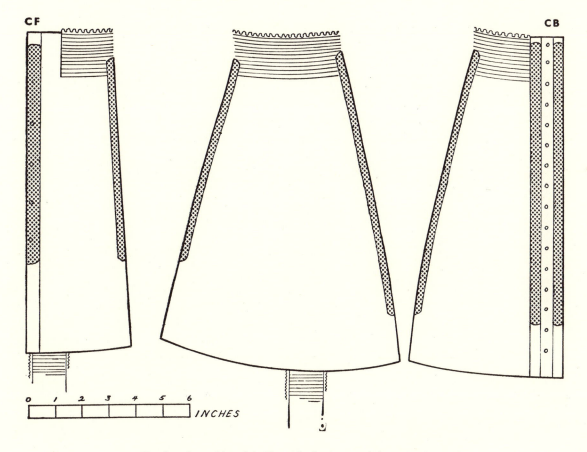

47 Peach-coloured broché silk with elastic round the waist (*c. 1918*)

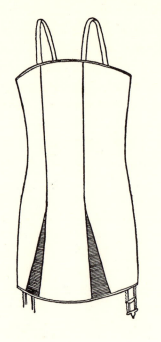
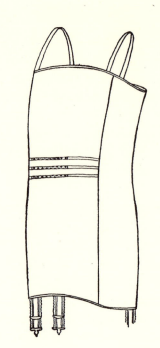

48 Corselet in thin pink cotton broché, with elastic insets. It fastens down the left side with hooks and eyes (*c. 1925*)

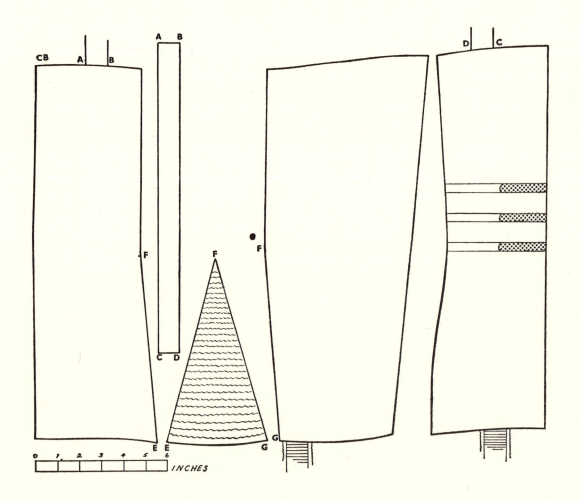

INCHES

a slight stretch, and finally in 1911 the first elastic belt; they were always very lightly boned and sometimes buttoned or hooked at the side so as to dispense with the front busk. These lighter corsets came into general wear during the war (47, 81) and only the older woman continued to wear the old-fashioned heavily boned coutil models. The change in underclothes continued, they were now very simply cut and delicately ornamented and made from the sheerest materials, light-weight silks, e.g. crêpe-de-chine, georgette, chiffon for luxury wear, otherwise thin cottons and voiles; pink became the favourite colour, a fashion which soon spread to the corsets and brassières—with these new under-garments a brassière was essential.

It took a few years for the fashion world and all its offshoots to recover from the war, and during that time the loose comfortable clothes—the straight "chemise" frocks—continued to be worn. As these dresses hung from the shoulders with no attempt to fit the body, comfort not shape became the guiding principle in choosing a corset. Most women had by now grown accustomed to this new-found freedom of movement, so perhaps it was not surprising that when, in 1921, a definite new fashion did emerge it was that of the immature girl who required no support. But the women who follow the fashion are not as a rule the immature schoolgirls, so once again the corsetière came to the rescue—this time to make the figure as shapeless as possible. The chemise dress became more fitting—if it had a waist, then it was on the hips—the problem was to hide the waist and eliminate all curves. By 1920 the corset, now only a belt, had reached the waist. This corset belt was very slightly shaped, an elastic waist-band and a few bones providing all the fitting considered necessary; more elastic was being used, whole panels of it often replacing the lacing, until finally an all-elastic belt, the "roll-on", often with no bones or lacing, captured the market. With all these a brassière was worn; it was made from a straight piece of material, very slightly darted and seamed at the side, sometimes also of elastic, its object being no longer to support but to flatten the bust and so eliminate all curves. Unfortunately on a plump figure between these two garments a roll of fat, known as the "tyre", would protrude to spoil the straight line. To flatten this tyre suspenders were added to the brassière so that it could be held down over the top of the corset belt; soon it was but a short step to combine the two, and the "corselette" was created. By cutting this garment perfectly straight and tethering it down all round with suspenders, thus pushing the breasts down and the stomach and hips up, from outside a beautiful uniform flatness was achieved (48, 85). The young woman, if possible, dispensed with all these garments and wore a suspender belt only; it must not be forgotten that twentieth-century education, with its accent on games and physical training, had by now produced a woman whose firm young body was adequately supported by her own muscles: "belts and bra's" were usually worn, the more mature adopted the corselette, and only the very, very old fashioned still wore whaleboned coutil. It was the passing-out of the corset which had begun a hundred years earlier (82–84).

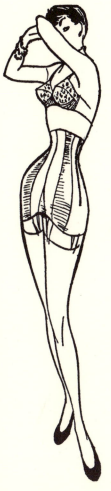

49 "Berlei" foundation: the return of the waist (1952)

It is tempting to glance beyond the scope of the present study, and see history repeating itself. In the early 1930's curves, very slight it is true, again appeared and yet once more the corsetière had to provide a foundation for a new line. Again a shapeless body garment had to be transformed, and this time with as little inconvenience to the wearer as possible. A new corset era has begun, a new name is given—"the foundation garment". The sixteenth/seventeenth-century corset had relied almost entirely on whalebone for shaping, the nineteenth/twentieth-century corset on whalebone plus cutting, the new corset almost entirely on cutting. These new foundation garments, expertly shaped in light-weight, non-stretching materials, e.g. nylon, combined with light-weight elastics, are worn directly on the body and have provided woman with a new "controlled" skin (49). Let us hope that the corsetière, having mastered these new materials, will allow women to keep their normal figure. But this new corset phase is still in its early stage and who can say what strange distortions of shape the artist-corsetière, inspired by his new technique, will devise for woman's malleable flesh?

2

THE CRINOLINE AND THE BUSTLE

The hip-pads, which were attached to the back of the dress at the end of the eighteenth century, continued to be worn at the beginning of the nineteenth century; they became much smaller, but remained as long as the high waists were worn. As the skirts increased in width in the 1830's the hip-pads, now called "bustles", became larger until finally they were discarded in favour of the stiffened petticoats. Various kinds of petticoats were tried out, but the most popular was that made of horse-hair (Fr. *crin*—horsehair) which appeared about 1839, and which gave its name to any artificial petticoat of the nineteenth century— "the crinoline".

Although muslins and light materials were very fashionable, during the first half of the nineteenth century they became much stiffer and crisper; silks were increasingly popular, but they too were of light weight and paper-like in quality. This type of material, together with the great vogue of the flounced skirt, required some kind of foundation; soon the horsehair petticoat was not sufficient, the number of petticoats increased, some reinforced with cording, some with whalebone, until eventually the problem of supporting the ever-increasing circumference of the skirt was at last solved in 1856 by the invention of a "cage" petticoat made of steel wires, very soon to be perfected by the use of "watch-spring" steel. While the fashion of the flounced skirt lasted the crinoline was dome-shaped, but to accommodate the simpler skirt of the sixties it flattened out in front, but became larger and spread out into a train behind—a fashion much more pleasant for the wearer, the inconvenience caused by the volume behind not being her affair (50, 75–80).

From 1866 the crinoline began to subside, and by 1867 the surplus material not yet discarded was arranged in elegant draperies. These in their turn required support, and so in 1868, though the crinoline had become very much smaller, it acquired additional steels in the waist at the back (51). This new form of the bustle was known by the more elegant French name "*tournure*" (93). A very much reduced crinoline was worn with it until well into the seventies; it might have the tournure attached, or have a separate one, worn on top of the crinoline. When the skirt got still narrower the crinoline was discarded and the tournure alone worn, until a new long slender line appeared; the dress moulded the figure in front and on the hips and the back draperies fell down behind into a long fan-like train (52). The very fashionable even discarded the tournure altogether, layers of flounces placed low down on the petticoat being considered sufficient (87).

The new, long line of the middle seventies was, however, too sudden a change for the average woman accustomed for centuries to hide her hips; she never entirely discarded the tournure and in the early eighties she began to arrange additional draperies to conceal her hips once more. This new tournure climbed up again, grew in volume, and this time stuck out from the waist almost at right angles from the centre back. 1885–1886 were the peak

50 Large crinoline of white cotton. The steels are only one-eighth of an inch wide and are hinged under the straight pieces, at the side back (*c. 1864*)

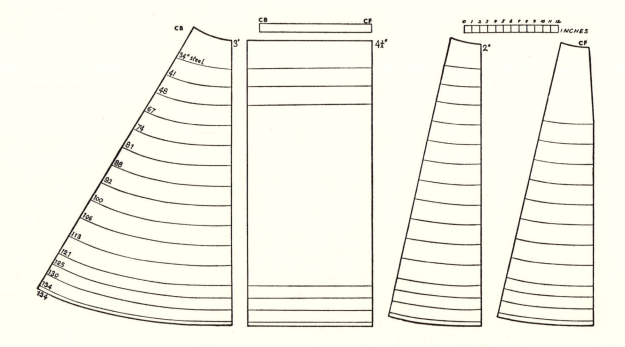

CB 3"

34" steel
41
48
67
74
81
88
92
100
106
113
121
125
130
134
134

CB   CF
4½"

0 1 2 3 4 5 6 7 8 9 10 11 12
INCHES

2"   CF

94

51 Small crinoline, with bustle
attached, of white cotton, dated
inside (*1872*)

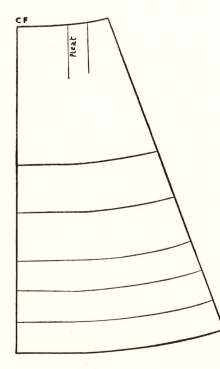

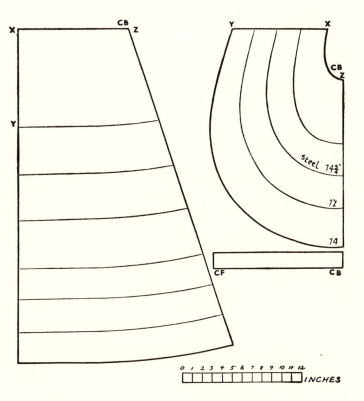

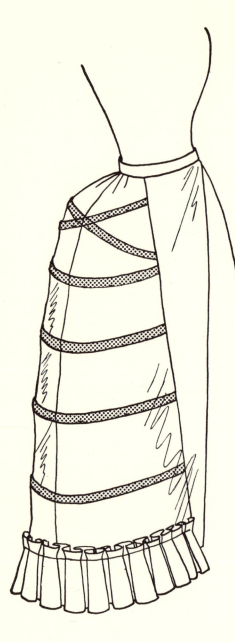

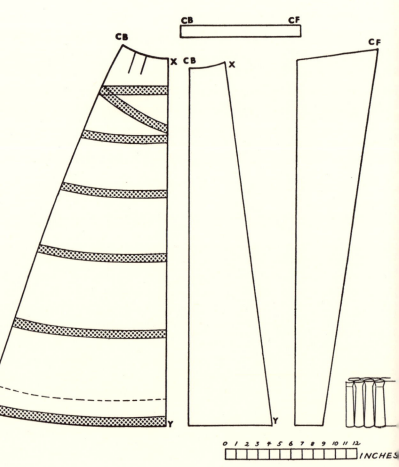

years for this particular tournure; from then on, owing to the simplification of the dress draperies, it began to dwindle, until at the end of the eighties it was only a mere horsehair pad attached inside the skirt, and then that too vanished. By 1890 the hips and behind had once more emerged, and this time to stay. A lady was no longer afraid to expose her figure, for it was provided, not by nature, but by a very expert corsetière.

As the nineteenth century advanced materials became stiffer and heavier. The early 1890's dresses had a sharply defined silhouette and were always mounted on a firm underlining. But with the discarding of the artificially supported petticoat the weight of the materials began to change; by the end of the century soft woollens, i.e. cashmere, soft silks (crêpe-de-chine and chiffon), had come in. For some time dress bodices were still mounted on a fitted whaleboned interlining, and skirts, though no longer interlined, were worn over stiff silk petticoats, but the accent all the time was on a softer line; gradually all linings were discarded and fabrics became still limper both for dresses and for underclothes, and eventually the straight chemise dress of the twenties was the result.

In recent years the increased use of synthetic raw materials has stiffened up dress fabrics considerably; there is also the inevitable swing back from the perpendicular line and the returning waist; all these will undoubtedly play an important part in influencing the future of the petticoat.

53 Petticoat of stiff silk or starched cotton, to be worn over a small crinoline, or without one (*1869*)

THE CORSET—FROM CONTEMPORARY MAGAZINES

During the Revolution the Athenian mode of attire was adopted. A French lady of that time gives the following account of it: "A simple piece of linen, slightly laced before, while it leaves the waist uncompressed, serves the purpose of a corset. If a robe is worn which is not open in front, petticoats are altogether dispensed with, the cambric chemise having the semblance of one, from its being trimmed with lace."   *The Book of Costume by a Lady of Rank*

January 1810

I recollect, when short waists were introduced, a physician, well known for the terseness and point of his medical aphorisms, observed that the ease and comfort which this mode of dress seemed to indicate was deceptive, for that beneath the Grecian flow of outline, was hidden a stiff corset, or armour of whalebone, which effectually counteracted the natural simplicity of the dress, and was in reality as destructive to health as the tight-laced stays, against which the physicians had so recently levelled their anatheme.

February 1810

I have seen, with considerable uneasiness, that stiff stays have been creeping in upon us gradually, and almost imperceptibly, till at length, concealment is no longer affected. Tired of being at ease, and ambitious of the sufferings and martyrdom of their grandmothers, our young ladies fearlessly advance to the torture of steel and whalebone, and willingly sacrifice their comfort and well being on what they conceive to be the shrine of elegance and taste.   ACKERMANN's *Repository of Arts*

January 1811

There have been many complaints against corsets: and ladies not only abandoned them, but, without dresses, without fichus, they went about practically in their chemises. From this extreme they have now fallen into the other. They not only tight-lace, encase themselves in whalebone busks as in days gone by, but the corsets are now longer and stronger than ever. The corset of today not only confines the stomach, waist and shoulders but encircles and restricts the bust in such a way that a lady so encased cannot move at all. The great ladies who appear so elegantly arrayed are much to be pitied! They cannot laugh, eat, bend or turn round. They can hardly breathe. The least sigh must break the lace and cause disaster to their toilette.

February 1811

To the Editor,

What did you dare to write, sir, in your January number? What an uproar has been raised among the fair sex by your article on corsets . . . No, sir, my corsets do not make the ladies who wear them look like Egyptian mummies. That might be true, of course, if I make them as you said, with a profusion of whalebone, and busks. Our ladies have too delicate a taste, too fine a sense, too sure an eye, not to be able to distinguish among the articles indispensible for their toilette, the one which will help their charms, uphold and define their figures. They are now wearing my corsets "à la Ninon" (54), those "in X", and many others of my invention with great success. . . .

Excuse me, sir, if I have taken up your time with a subject which is my special concern, but it is also one of much interest to the fair sex,

I am, yours, etc., etc.,

Bretel, manufacturer, with diploma, of corsets

Journal des Dames et des Modes

December 1811

Of all the new inventions, perhaps the most popular and most talked of is that of elastic braces. The "old young" disguise the size of their stomach with an elastic belt; the faded coquettes support their fallen allurements with an elastic corset, the stockings of an *incroyable* are held up by an elastic garter, the elbow gloves of a pretty woman are attached by an elastic bracelet . . . It is as if a clever artist is playing with dolls that only move with springs (100).

Journal des Dames et des Modes

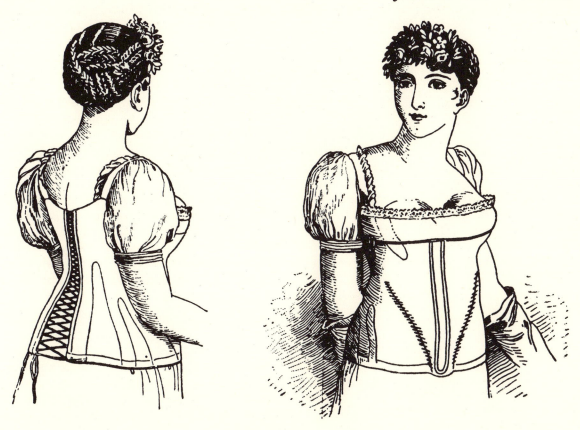

54   Corset *à la Ninon* (1810)

1811

We shall next speak of the stays, or corsets. They must be light and flexible, yielding to the shape, while they support it . . .

The bosom, which nature has formed with exquisite symmetry in itself, and admirable adaption to the parts of the figure to which it is united, has been transformed into a shape, and transplanted to a place, which deprives it of its original beauty and harmony with the rest of the person. This hideous metamorphose has been effected by means of newly invented stays or corsets which, by an extraordinary construction and force of material, force the figure of the wearer into whatever form the artist pleases. . . . In consequence we see, in eight women out of ten, the hips squeezed into a circumference little more than the waist; and the bosom shoved up to the chin, making a sort of fleshy shelf, disgusting to the beholders, and certainly most incommodious to the bearer.

Curiosity may incline you to wish to know something of these buckram machines, that you may form an idea of their intention, use, or rather inutility. I will satisfy you by describing them to the best of my power . . .

The first ("pregnant stay") is a corset or stay of dimity, or jean or silk; reaching from the shoulders, down the waist, and over the hips, to the complete envelopement of the body. It is rendered of more than ordinary power by elastic bones, etc., which introduced between the lining and covering of the stay, bring it to something like the consistence and shape of an ancient warrior's hauberk. This new-fashioned coat-of-mail for the fair sex is so constructed as to compress and reduce to the shape desired the natural prominence of the female figure in a state of fruitfulness . . .

The next ill-named thing I have to describe is the article of apparel called the "divorce". This title is even more shocking than the foregoing . . . It consists of a piece of steel or iron, of a triangular form, gently curved on each side. This formidable breast-plate (for the attraction of love's arrows, not to repel them!) is covered with soft materials; and thus bedded, placed in the centre of the chest to divide the breasts . . .

On the "long stay" I shall now make a few remarks, arising from the observations I have been enabled to make on the ladies of various ages and figures whom I have known wear it. To the woman whose waning charms set in an exuberance of flesh, perhaps the support of this adventitious aid is an advantage. But in that case its stiffening should rather be cord quilted in the lining, or very thin whale-bone, than either steel or iron. In all situations the bodice should be flexible to the motion of the body, and the undulations in the shape; and it should never be felt to press upon any part.

Thus far we may tolerate the adoption of this buckram suit for elderly or excessively en bon point ladies; but for the growing girl (who, I am sorry to say, mothers not unfrequently imprison in these machines) it is both unrequired and mischievous. . . . Let then the "long stay" be restricted to the too abundant mass of fattening matronhood; so may art restrain the excesses, not of nature, but of disease . . . Let the "padded corset" rectify the defects of the deformed. But where nature has given the outline of a well-constructed form, forbear to traverse her designs. Youth should be left to spring up unconfined like the young cedar; and when the hand of man, or accident, does not distort the pliant stem, it will grow erect and firm, spreading its beautiful and cheerful shade over the heads of its planters.
The Mirror of the Graces

April 1816

We have been favoured with the sight of a new stay, the "corset des Grâces", which we understand has received very distinguished patronage. This stay possesses the double advantage of improving the shape, and conducing towards the preservation of the health; no compression, no pushing the form out of its natural proportions; it allows the most perfect ease and freedom to every motion, while, at the same time, it gives that support to the frame, which delicate women find absolutely necessary.
ACKERMANN'S *Repository of Arts*

February 1820

It is sad and afflicting to be condemned to the ball-dress of the present day. I abhor the long waists, the miserable busks, and the whale-bone, that carry us back to I know not what Gothic period. Certainly excessively short waists were ungraceful, because it rendered the women ill-made, and they were all hump-backed. But is there not a middle point, and is not the Grecian the just and unchanging model of grace and beauty? But what avails remonstrance? Silly vanity governs us—tyrant fashion is superior to reason, and we must follow the torrent.
Journal des Modes

February 1825

A modern writer, after remarking that the beauty of the waist, whether high, intermediate, or low, depends in a great measure in the form of the corsets or stays, thus expresses himself:

The great fault of corsets or stays is, that however extended and supported both before and behind,

PATENT-BOLSTERS:— *Le moyen d'etre en bon point*.

55 **1791.** "The bosom, which Nature planted at the bottom of her chest, is pushed up by means of wadding and whalebone to a station so near her chin that in a very full subject that feature is sometimes lost between the invading mounds."

From a contemporary caricature

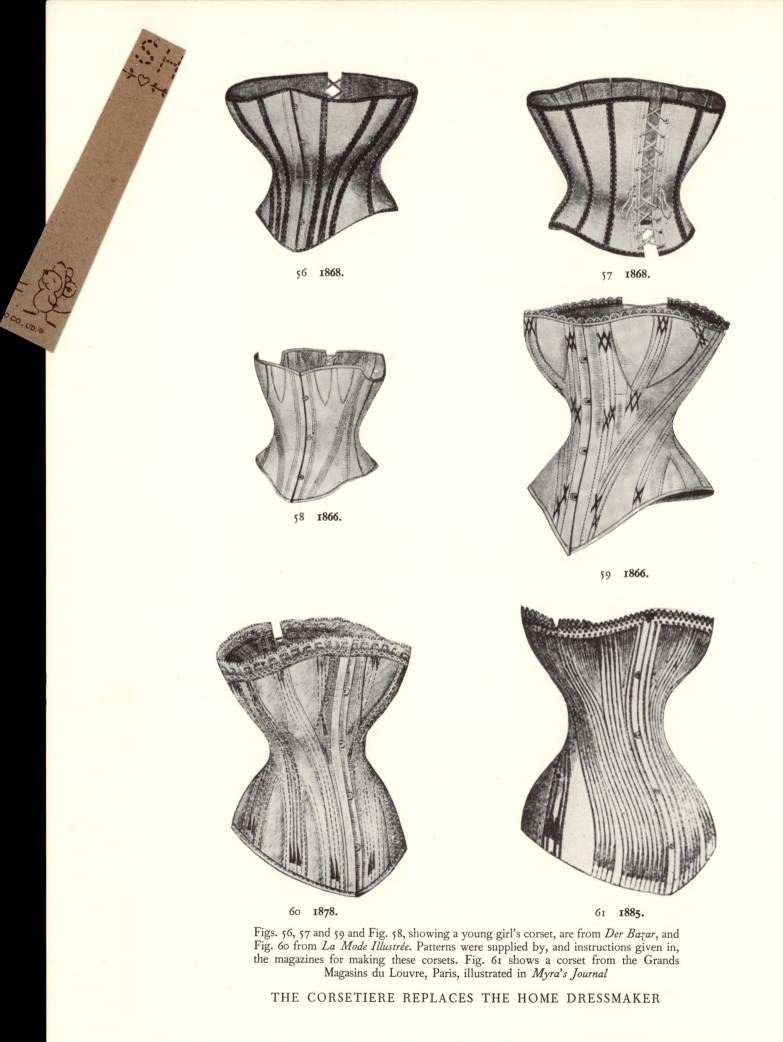

56 **1868.**

57 **1868.**

58 **1866.**

59 **1866.**

60 **1878.**

61 **1885.**

Figs. 56, 57 and 59 and Fig. 58, showing a young girl's corset, are from *Der Bazar*, and Fig. 60 from *La Mode Illustrée*. Patterns were supplied by, and instructions given in, the magazines for making these corsets. Fig. 61 shows a corset from the Grands Magasins du Louvre, Paris, illustrated in *Myra's Journal*

THE CORSETIERE REPLACES THE HOME DRESSMAKER

they want both extension and support on the sides. They consequently fall into pleats, which at once pinch the sides, and gradually destroy the beauty of the form of the corsets themselves. A little consideration of the shape will shew, that in the back of the stays extension throughout is chiefly wanted; in the front, extension throughout and pressure inferiorly perhaps; and on the sides extension throughout, pressure or support above, towards the bosom, perhaps, and adaption or pliability chiefly in the middle and below.

The extension throughout the back should be produced by two thin steels in the lower and middle third of the back, and by a stiff cord of cotton continued from the steel throughout the upper third.

The extension throughout the front, and the pressure, if necessary, to repress any prominence inferiorly, should be produced by a tempered steel of at least two inches wide, bent inward into a semicircular form, and sufficiently long to extend over the prominence.

The extension, support, and pliability on the sides, should be produced by two means—first, a tempered steel about half an inch wide, and extending from the end of the shoulderstrap downward and forward—over the outer or posterior part of the bosom, and over the side; and secondly, a piece let in on the side, extending from the arm-pit over the hip, and rendered elastic by transverse springwires, not more than half an inch apart.

This apparatus may be termed the basis or skeleton of the stays; and all the rest ought to be formed on this by very small but closely filled cords of cotton, except in such directions as the peculiar form of the individual might require small slips of bone.

The shape of the bosom ought not to be formed by gores, but by two half cones very finely and closely cottoned so as to give a firm support. The shoulderstraps should be elastic.

Some useful hints may possibly be derived from these remarks; but the employment of steel, so extensively recommended, appears to me extremely objectionable, on the score of health as well as of ease and comfort.   *La Belle Assemblée*

1827

A very elegant lady I once knew used to place two wide cotton ribbons on the straight of the material of the stomach gussets of her corsets and these ribbons then went through a cotton buckle sewn to each stocking. This kind of garter was to keep the corset from riding up on the hips, and also dispensed with wearing the usual garters which are bad for the circulation of the blood.
                                                                                                      Manuel des Dames

December 1828

We are sorry to record (because we know of a very recent instance of its becoming fatal) the practice of pinching in the waist, by extreme tight lacing, to a slenderness, as unnatural as it is disagreeable, and unpleasing to the sight. This hideous and wasp-like fashion still prevails.
                                                                                                      La Belle Assemblée

March 1831

Mrs Bell's house has long been unrivalled for the elegance of its corsets, which boast those advantages so rarely united, of strengthening and supporting the frame, and adding singular grace to the shape. A recent discovery enables Mrs Bell to extend these advantages still farther by substituting India rubber for elastic wires. The rubber is manufactured in strong and delicate fibres, which possess all the elasticity of wire, without being like it subject to snap, or corrode.   *World of Fashion*

December 1834

The most elegant Ladies have adopted Corsets without shoulder straps and without whalebone; for full toilette these Corsets are made of white poux de soie.   *Townsend's Parisian Fashions*

December 1836

Corsets Josselin: Among the many new inventions with which industry has enriched fashion these last few years, none can be more recommended than that of the "Corsets Josselin", whose merits and enormous advantages have been sanctioned by various reports from learned societies and by the medals awarded to M. Josselin, sole inventor of these corsets, which have become the indispensible foundation of all toilettes. To understand this success it is only necessary to look at the ingenious contrivance by which a simple and delicate mechanism, placed beside the eyelet holes, allows for lacing or unlacing the corset without help from a second person, and also without disturbing the dress—the laces widen by pressing the finger on a little button. There is another convenient system to take off the corset, which can be quickly undone by a simple spring placed on the front of the corset. No other invention is so pleasant and useful as it means one can dress and undress unaided in less than a second.

Petit Courrier des Dames

February 1837

(Advertisement.) Madame George's Corset "à la Bayadère" has now been introduced to English Ladies, and where it has become known it has for ever superseded every other. Its ease, simplicity, and elegance are at once so apparent, when placed beside the whalebone Machines which excruciate the body, distort the figure, and destroy the health; its efficacy in giving a small and graceful roundness to the waist which decreased it to the eye without any real compression is instantaneous! Madame has also invented a new CALISTHENIC CORSET, totally devoid of bone, in which young ladies can with ease perform the most difficult of Calisthenic exercises. *Townsend's Parisian Fashions*

1841

The modern stay extends not only over the bosom but also all over the abdomen and back down to the hips; besides being garnished with whalebone to say nothing of an immense wooden, metal, or whalebone, busk passing in front from the top of the stays to the bottom; they have been growing in length by degrees; the gait of an Englishwoman is generally stiff and awkward there being no bend or elasticity of the body on account of the form of her stays. *Handbook of the Toilet*

April 1843

Corsets Josselin: Corset "à la Watteau". The corsets "Watteau" are continuing their success when worn with summer toilettes, and their only disadvantage we say is that they make last year's dresses impossible to wear because they make the body much longer and the waist much slimmer.

Petit Courrier des Dames

February 1844

Madame Dumoulin's corsets without gussets have been attracting attention. Their cut is very advantageous to the figure, they do not interfere with breathing and they liberate the hips. They are made of from seven up to thirteen pieces, according to the size; these pieces decrease and increase gradually so as to follow the contours of the figure much better than an English corset or one with gussets. It is a complete revolution from the former cut, and Madame Dumoulin richly deserves the diploma she has received; she is a real creator for she has suppressed the gussets, and replaced them by the seven to thirteen separate pieces which are arranged so as not to construct the figure and yet be free from wrinkles. *Les Modes Parisiennes*

October 1848

(Advertisement.) *Rational Corsets*: There is a new application of caoutchouc, which is introduced in the form of fine threads covered with lace-thread, into the staple of the cloth of which stays are made. Such a mode of introducing this material, it will be seen, permits of free evaporation; while the elasticity obtained does away with the necessity for whalebone, except in such thin flakes as can do no harm. In the ease with which an elastic ligature like this yields to the motions of the chest, consists of course its great superiority over the old corsets; but the perfect adaption of the new invention to the shape and the graceful flexibility it permits to the figure, will, we suspect, be considered still greater advantages by the wearer. The inventors are Messrs. Thomas & Co. of Cheapside, London.

Townsend's Parisian Fashions

March 1855

Among the most successful creations of the Industrial Exhibition of course we would point out a new cut, called the "Ceinture Créole"—it has no shoulder straps, no gussets at the bust, it is just a simple arrangement of shapes to give health and elegance. The "Ceinture Créole" is above all suitable for young figures whose development should suffer no compression. This invention is the nearest approach to antique beauty—we should not admire the beautiful antique statues if they wore whale-bones and busks.
Petit Courrier des Dames

January 1868

Thomson's Glove-Fitting Corset: In dress, everything depends upon the corset; no dress, however well made, can fit a figure properly if the corset does not . . . Thomson's Corset is cut on a principle different from those hitherto in vogue. It is in three pieces, the centre front forms a Swiss belt, the upper and lower parts gradually increase in size. There is a peculiarity in the lacing at the back, in itself a recommendation to a corset. The laces cross and pass through two holes opposite the usual eyelet-holes, and the lace can be fastened in front, or, if tied at the back, the bow or knot is not felt in the least. A new and exceedingly simple fastening secures the front, and a concealed spring prevents the opening of the lowest stud, which not unfrequently occurs in common stays. The name "Glove-Fitting" is certainly well-chosen, for these things do fit "like a glove".

December 1868

If we could, as the American lady expressed it, be melted and poured into our stays, there would be hope for all, but since this is not attainable under the existing regime, let us see what is the next best. Suppose our stays could be moulded to our figures! Suppose that each individual lady could have every pair of corsets she buys moulded to her own form, and this without trouble or unreasonable expense! This is done, is a fait accompli! Messrs Johnson, Hatchman & Co., have invented and patented a corset which is moulded by steam upon lay figures of metal and earthenware; each lay figure is modelled from the most beautiful types of the "female form divine", and is made in every size, from the tiny waist of the extremest tight-lacer to the comfortable figure of the elderly matron. The peculiarity in the cut of the "Line of Beauty" corset is that the back, instead of being, as usual, cut straight, is curved at the waist, thus allowing the stay to fall well into the back, and giving the round appearance to the waist which is the chief characteristic of a "good figure". The stay is moulded to the figure and fits at once, instead of only falling to the lines of the form after some weeks' wear.
Englishwoman's Domestic Magazine

July 1874

One remarkable trait of present modes is, that bodices are made much longer-waisted than they have been for some years past. Much greater attention is also paid to the elegance of a small waist, than was the case with former styles of costumes. A long body requires a slight waist, and so your English amateurs of tight lacing are likely to be grateful once more. The very short corsets worn by Parisiennes of late years, are probably doomed soon to go out of favour, and many a lady of fashion has already exchanged it for a longer and firmer support to the figure (59). *The Young Englishwoman*

June 1875

I have been for some time seeking for a house keeping all the corsets of repute manufactured, and I have succeeded in my search. Mrs. Adley Bourne, of 37, Picadilly, keeps every kind of good corset made. To begin with, Thomson's Glove-Fitting and other celebrated corsets; Izod's steam-shaped corsets, perfect alike in form and wearing qualities; French wove corsets, for small neat figures; Gazelin's Paris-wove and other makes, and now the well-known Swanbill corset, especially designed for wearing under the cuirasse bodice, and well suited for stout figures. The Swanbill Corset has a busk longer than that of the ordinary corset; the shape is indicated by the name. The Swanbill is most effective in reducing the figure and keeping the form flat, so as to enable ladies, otherwise too rounded in outline, to wear the fashionable vetements of the day . . . Many ladies now wear all their jupons beneath

62. French wove corset and petticoat of Surat silk. From an advertisement of Mrs Adley Bourne's Ladies' Warehouse (*1890*)

the long-fronted corset, in order to allow the tight corsage to "set" well. Mrs Bourne, to meet this mode, has her new jupons nicely banded so as to allow of their being worn with comfort under the corset. All her new petticoats are scanty, and fulness thrown to the back.

Myra's Journal

1876

Fashion is inflexible on one point, ladies must be slender. So much the worse for those who if among the trials and tribulations of this world they suffer from too much flesh. Poor victims! I am really sorry for them, for if they will follow the fashions they must be encased in a sheath. Some have special corsets made for them. In former days corsets generally stopped at the waist; now they are divided into two parts, and there is an under corset for the stomach—to say nothing of the very heavy busk which stretches from top to bottom of the two parts. The cuirasse-corsage now moulds not only the waist but encloses the whole figure from top to bottom.

La Mode Illustrée

March 1877

The cuirasse corsage is longer than ever, and is not only whaleboned at every seam, but has small lead weights, enclosed in silk and quite flat, sewn in the lining at front, back and hips.

October 1878

I am convinced that the Duchesse Corset is one of the best and most suitable models for stout figures. The busks are very long, tapering and flexible at the top, but exceedingly strong from the waist to the edge. On each side of the corset, from the waist to the edge in front, a series of bones set in close together in a slanting direction, form a frame, which compresses the figure without injurious pressure; the corset is cut short, and rounded over the hips, to leave full play to the limbs, and to avoid the disagreeable creasing in this part.

Myra's Journal

1878

Let us have moderation and good taste. If an emaciated woman pad her dress, she must not overdo it, or pad it in the wrong place—that outrages nature more than if she left it alone.

The Art of Beauty

March 1881

"The cry is still, they come!", they, in this instance, being corsets with special adaptions of belts and other contrivances for improving the figure. "The International Corset" is one of the latest of these models, and has some improvements which will render it of more permanent efficacy than many other makes. There is very little doubt that in a great number of cases, what is specially required in a corset is the power of gradually tightening and drawing back the lower part without affecting the upper part; this is done by means of an additional belt springing from the hips and fastened at the back by means of a buckle or lacing, but everything depends upon the proper shape and adjustment of the belt. If not very carefully made it rubs up out of place, or if cut too straight the lower part fits the figure while the upper part forms gaps standing out stiffly and forming unsightly lumps or knobs under the dress. In the "International Corset" these drawbacks have been avoided.

63 **1898.** "Corset Tailleur", coutil, 7s. 11d. (*Peter Robinson*)

64 **1899.** "Swanbill" corset, black coutil, £1 10s. (*Adley Bourne*)

65 **1900.** "Spécialité" corset. The new straight-fronted corset, white coutil, 27s. 6d. (*Dickins and Jones*)

66 **1900.** "Spécialité" corset, (*Dickins and Jones*)

67 **1907.** Corset in white coutil, 15s. 9d. (*Royal Worcester*)

68 **1908.** Ribbon corset, 1s. 11½d. (*Spiers and Ponds*)

FROM "WASP-WAIST" TO "S-CURVE"

69 **1902.** The "Erect Form" corset "follows the natural outlines of the form and does not compress the figure into a graceless illogical shape." (*Weingarten Bros.*)

70 **1908.** The "Spécialité" corset—"a new form designed to give those straight lines so essential to the present style of dress." (*Dickins and Jones*)

THE "S-CURVE" BEGINS TO STRAIGHTEN

June 1881

The Louvre corsets include every variety of make; the most stylish are of satin, the dress fitting without a wrinkle over this lovely and durable material . . . Summer corsets of tulle with very light whalebone, suitable for India—those ladies who suffer in warm weather will do well to have a pair of these corsets in reserve (44).

. . . by the staymaker, and in these days of wondrous corsets . . . wrong they will follow their own sweet will as surely as water runs down . . . ich measure round the waist two inches less than the nude waist will generally be found perfectly fitting and pleasant to wear. Some figures require more hip room than the ready-made corsets allows; in this case the wearers must either have their corsets made for them or else wear them a little open at the back. If the hips are not well developed it is not difficult to place a little cotton wool inside the corset and fill the space with this soft material.

February 1884

The narrow busk is again coming into favour, and it certainly has much to recommend it.

However conservative we women are in our ways, and habits, there is one innovation we have all adopted; the suspender in place of the old-fashioned garter.

June 1884

Good and well developed figures are, as all who have had any experience of dressmaking know, very much easier to fit than those of very slender proportions, and devices of all kinds to improve the defects of nature have from time immemorial been in use by our sex, always striving to arrive at perfection. The latest, and amongst the most necessary aids of the kind that I have seen, are the Bust Improvers introduced by Messrs. Worth et Cie. These Bust Improvers are rightly so termed, for they are calculated to improve figures of defective outline as well as to give roundness to those that are too slim for our present ideas of beauty and fashion.

July 1891

Broché silks are the most fashionable materials for corsets, and they are lined with silk or linen. For summer wear, corsets are being made of an open, net-like fabric over coloured silk, and some ball dresses are accompanied by corsets made of the same material, as the dress. A bodice of some kind is always worn over the corset, not so much to protect this as to soften its hard outline under the dress. Bodices are made of cambric, nainsook, the finest longcloth or surah. Many ladies, however, prefer, as ensuring a more perfect fit, woven bodies in silk or lisle thread, which cling to the figure and mould like jersey.   *Myra's Journal*

1891

Everyone cannot wear a garter as tight as it should be. Their legs swell under pressure, and varicose veins form. In this case the stockings should be fastened to the stays by ribbons (suspenders). But accidents might happen; for if the ribbon, which must be well stretched to hold up the stockings were to break, down comes the stocking over the heel! What a catastrophe! My advice is to wear at the same time a garter not at all tight, but sufficiently so to hold up the stocking, in case of accidents, until the damage can be repaired. To wear the garter below the knee is against all rules of taste.

The Lady's Dressing Room

December 1892

No one at the present day with any regard for their health and comfort dreams of wearing garters, those instruments of torture, which to be useful must be too tight for comfort, and if bearably loose cause untold anxieties lest they should become looser still. Of the substitutes for garters that I have seen I give preference to the suspenders supplied with Hoven's Clip, which does not tear the stocking and holds it firmly and safely in its grasp.   *Myra's Journal*

July 1898

In Paris, tight frocks have become the rule which outline the contour—may it be called—so mercilessly, thin women have found that the addition of false hips assists them most satisfactorily to that consumation of good figure which they so devoutly desire. Accordingly, a great demand for these articles of "bijouterie et vertu" has arisen, penetrating to even our own highly developed West End, where the motto of "Nature unadorned, adorned the most", certainly no longer obtains. "Yet, what is one to do?" as an artificially assisted damsel declared in my presence some days since; "it must be rounded art or angular Nature, and of the two commend me to the former"—which, indeed, is monstrous wisdom on the lips of two-and-twenty. *The Sketch*

September 1900

Our readers have for a long time past appreciated the merits of the "Specialité" corsets, which are sold exclusively by Dickens & Jones, of Regent Street, and this enterprising firm which is always well to the fore with all the latest novelties, has now added to the series a new straight-fronted corset. It is one on the lines of the very latest Paris corsets, which have been designed expressly for wearing with the fashionable skirts fitting closely round the hips. It will be seen that this beautiful corset is cut low in front, so that an absolutely natural appearance is preserved at the bust, but its leading characteristic is a perfectly straight busk, which keeps the figure flat in front below the waist, and reduces all tendency to embonpoint . . . Being cut low in front it is as comfortable to sit in as to stand in (65).

January 1901

It is rather curious to find that the crusade against the corset that doctors and physiologists generally have waged for so long should be crowned with success. Not that there is any prospect of the corset being abolished; that is neither possible nor desirable; but the garment has been practically revolutionised, so that it supports the figure without compressing it.

The Lady

February 1901

We are beginning to realise that our "all too solid flesh" will not melt, that if we send it away from its legitimate moorings it will appear somewhere; if our waists are unduly small the figure below the waist becomes out of proportion. Now we are learning to adopt a stay, when we have passed the heydey of youth and sylph-like slimness of girlhood, which gives room for our bodies without spoiling our appearance, by lengthening the waist and slightly enlarging it. Imitation is the sincerest flattery, and these styles, which formerly only found a place among the very best corsets in France and England, are now being reproduced in all the cheapest makes. No fashionable woman need tight lace; she is required to present an unbroken line from the décolletage to the knee, and this prevents any undue drawing in of the waist line, but the adoption is by no means universal. Many of our fashionable dressmakers still keep to the old style and the curve at the waist line. *The Queen*

February 1902

The little Empire corset—or ceinture—merely covers the bust, and is held by shoulder straps, and over this the Empire toilette hangs to perfection. Then for the figure with hips inclined to spread unduly there are many new basque corsets, where the hips are completely covered by a shaped basque, put on separately, and held down by double or triple sets of suspenders.

October 1902

Corsets are made straighter fronted than ever. Waists are considered trifles to which all sensible women have said good-bye. *The Lady*

1902

An upright poise of the shoulders, long sloping bust with straight front line and a graceful curve over the hips. The waist held in well below the figure; the chest carried well forward and the shoulders down; the waist long in front and short behind. *The Lady's Realm*

October 1903

There seems every probability that the great corset question will assert itself once more ere long, after being more or less in abeyance since the advent of the sensible straight-front corset, for some of the new types that are presented are quite as exaggerated in their way, and quite as opposed to the laws alike of hygiene and art, as were the obsolete "hour-glass" corsets (67, 69).

One of the latest designs is not a corset proper, but a corselet and hip protector, made entirely of woven purse silk, which while being quite supple and elastic still supports the figure and gives a neat outline, the only stiffening being the front fastening steels, and bones to keep the laces in place at the back. It can be worn with or without the bust bodice, which, however, is extremely comfortable and is boned at the sides and back to retain its shapeliness. This bust bodice is often worn also over an ordinary corset. (From an advertisement of Debenham & Freebody.)

October 1904

Note-worthy among the ready-made models are an elastic ribbon corset that is eminently comfortable wear, especially for athletic girls, affording really efficient support to the waist (46, 68).

November 1905

Although Empire fashions are the latest mode, yet they require so much "dressing-up" so that they do not suit the majority of wearers. With an Empire evening gown the ordinary corset is impossible, but the short Empire corset is not sufficient for any but the most slender figure. A corset with a fashionable waist and too defined hips ruins the set of an Empire gown, but the straight natural corset, with few bones and a buttoned front, is admirable, and the dress is not creased into a waistline when dancing with the average man who holds his partner by the waist, despite the waistless garment.

The Lady

March 1907

"The Human Form Divine and How it Follows the Fashion"—One of the many tirades of men on the subject of the follies of women asserts that we change the outline of our figure almost as often as we do our minds . . . we have always been allowed to change our minds, and we have taken it as a matter of right that we should change our figures also if we were so pleased. Now we are expected to have our waist either at the true waist line or to be what is called short-waisted. Indeed, with the craze for Empire fashions there would seem to be an inclination for the defining line between bust and hips to come higher and higher, and perhaps we may in time adopt the mode of the early part of the nineteenth century, when the waist of a bodice simply enclosed the bust . . . Within the past few years very long waists have been in vogue, and straight fronts threatened to do away with waists altogether . . . Empire fashions do not lend themselves to prominent hips. Happily the corsetière of to-day is a very potent contributor to beauty culture, and meets all these difficulties by her clever stays . . . Many of the beauty culturists make stays a part of their business, and those who are troubled with big hips, which interfere with the present fashion, can reduce them by exercises, and half an hour in the morning must be sacrificed to a good cause. But, of course, it is an acknowledged axiom "qu'il faut souffrir pour être belle."

Those of us who have seen the iron prison under the name of stays in which young women a couple of centuries ago were locked see a great resemblance between those modes and the modes of to-day in stays. They are longer than they have ever been—certainly six or ten inches longer now than they used to be on the hips. The lacings are taut and straight, so well-developed women must study their figures with diligence. Some of the new corsets lace both back and front. But there is a choice of figures. The Princess and the Empire both demand diametrically different forms, the one long-waisted, and the other very short.

The Queen

November 1908

"*The New Directoire Corset.*" It is curious (and incidentally rather amusing) to note how, meek as a lamb, every woman who aims at observing the various phases of Fashion will adapt herself to its idiosyncrasies. In some cases the marked peculiarities involved are of doubtful advantage, but the present very striking vogue, which demands a complete alteration of one's figure, can command nothing but praise. The hygienically disposed will learn with approval that there is no "squeezing in" of the waist in this instance. Indeed, there is a definite loosening of the corset in that region, for the simple reason that curves are strictly eschewed with the Directoire sheath-like gown. Obviously, therefore, it is a straight-up-and-down effect about which the corsetières have been busying themselves, and a long-perfectly-moulding corset is positively the only way to achieve this.

March 1910

To be flatly contradicted when she asserts that the prevailing waist-measurement is larger, though the general effect is considerably slimmer, should constitute for the modern corsetière the greatest compliment in the world. She achieves her effect by means of corsets of extreme length, that, while girding up the figure quite low down (and thereby imparting an effect of straight-frontedness, with slender hips), leave the region of the waist and, by so doing, all the important organs absolutely unrestricted. This waist latitude becomes absolutely necessary, by the way, as it is anatomically absurd to pretend that the cleverest corsetière in the world can completely spirit away all trace of "superfluity".

The Lady

March 1911

"*The New Figure*." This may, I think, be called the Poiret figure, for it is certainly in his salons that the boneless corset is most in vogue. Naturally, no society woman will turn herself into a pillow-shaped bundle for anyone in the world, but she will have to renounce her waist-line if she wishes to have the silhouette "à la mode". Most Englishwomen dislike the idea extremely, for they still love the small waist, and they say Englishmen do also. And yet the small waist is such a snare for physical ills! The Frenchwoman does not cling to slimness in the same way. She likes a fine line, but it need not mean a tiny waist. She looks at the length from shoulder to heel, and she avoids trimming as much as possible. Moreover she is very careful that her corset shall be made to follow the long lines in her own particular figure, and she wears a soutien-gorge to keep her shoulders back.

"*Our Dress Prospects*." Very certainly we are condemned to narrow skirts, short waists, and garments cut in a fashion which makes last year's démodé and those of the year before quite impossible ... There is nothing encouraging in the changes which the season brings, as far as the well-developed are concerned, and it needs a strong woman with a strong chest, to cope with the paucity of garments which the cut of our gowns entails.

The Queen

August 1911

No busks, stiff or otherwise, and no lacing at back. These points single out the New Sports Corset, of the Knitted Corset Co., as conductive to supple ease of movement, made of a simple perfectly porous, flexible canvas fabric, supplemented by elastic, this corset is pliable, yet never "sloppy", being fitted with unbreakable spiral steels, which by the way, are removable to allow of washing ... For the river, for holiday wear, for country tramps, for lounging in garden chairs, as for tea gown wear, and even for the afternoon frock and tailor made, this dainty corset provides a most elegant and all sufficient basis if the wearer be fairly slim.

September 1912

Corsets are still fashioned very deep over the hips, to accord with the youthful slightness decreed by fashion. For a low cut at the bust the long-contoured feeling prevails, producing an appearance of naturalness, youth and elegance hitherto undreamt of. A brassière is usually worn in addition providing a supple, dainty extension of utmost value in consideration of the contour of the gown or costume, and as much in request with the extremely thin (for whom it conduces actually to "form" the figure), as it certainly is a necessity for those of generous build.

71   **1912.** Corset belt of the finest elastic, £3 13s. 6d. (*London Corset Co. Ltd.*)

72   **1913.** "De Bevoise" brassiere, 6s. 11d.

73   **1914.** French evening brassière, 12 fr. 50

74   **1918.** Corset in white coutil, 16s. 11d. (*J.B. Foundations*)

THE "EMPIRE" LINE

75 *c.* **1856.** Horsehair crinoline

76 **1858.** Cotton crinoline

77 **1860.** Cotton crinoline

78 **1864.** Cage crinoline

79 **1862.** Crinoline with horsehair flounce

80 **1866.** Cage crinoline with patent draw-string

THE CORSET—FROM CONTEMPORARY MAGAZINES

August 1913

Incomparably supple are Madame Soumis Corsets. Their extreme length and their straightness of line, without which it would be impossible to show deference to the present mode, go hand-in-hand with absolute freedom and a slimness only obtainable with a "glove-fitting" basis. This the "Corset Gaine" provides, as, although practically devoid of bone, it is fashioned from an exclusive fabric called the "Gaine" tricot material, which clings flat and never creases or gathers into rucks—retains its shape, in fact, until the corset is worn out. The corset fourreau in question is made of a special seamless material, light and soft; not likely to stretch. There is a bone at each side and that is all.

March 1915

A pretty bust bodice or a brassière now counts quite as much an essential as the corset so fine now and extremely devoid of superfluous folds and insertion and ribbon adornment, is the lingerie, and so low-cut the corset, that (one has it on the expert authority of the corsetière of Messrs Swan & Edgar's) even with the camisole, the addition of a dainty bust bodice is more often than not regarded as necessary to the equipment. On the other hand, the brassière usually supersedes the camisole, and is therefore greatly in demand among women who are other than slim, as, while dispensing with the extra garment, it also moulds the figure gracefully.

February 1919

Waists are a negligible quantity; there is rarely a suggestion of one, and most new models are cut on straight lines.

May 1919

It is sometimes argued that, with the "natural" figure in vogue, the need for care in corseting is minimised. Yet quite the contrary is the case. For whereas in the old days of tight-lacing and closely boned bodices, a large share in the responsibility for the appearance was borne by the dress itself, now it is quite otherwise, and unless a due degree of support is given beneath the bodice, the pretty dégagées lines can only degenerate into slovenliness. *The Lady*

May 1921

The low-placed waist is one of the outstanding features of new frocks.

The Queen

November 1921

Warner's "Corselette". The Warner Corselette combines a bandeau, an abdominal confiner, and four hose supporters in such a way to give an unbroken line from shoulder to knee. As a Corset House we know, and as Corset Wearers you know that no figure can long dispense with a corset and keep its lines. Yet there are figures and there are occasions which require less corsetry than others. We have developed for such occasions the Warner Corselette.

October 1923

The New "Combinaire" Corset. This "Combinaire Corset" is brassière and corset all in one, and is made from high grade porous and washable embroidered batiste. The simple fastening down front makes it easy to put on, and the back being closed with inserted elastic, an elegant silhouette is assured. The garment is particularly suitable for hot weather wear, the bones and suspenders easily removed for washing. *The Lady*

January 1923

Until fairly recently one had to decide definitely to be either corseted or uncorseted. Now there is a compromise—and that compromise exactly suits the requirements of the woman of fashion. Every woman would prefer, in view of the present loose, slim mode, to go uncorseted like the girl of sixteen,

81. Wick's Special "Sports" Corset
—The lighter type of corset which
became so popular; in 1913 it is advertised as suitable for the "Tango", in
1914 for Nursing and Red Cross
Work. Price, 13/9 (1913)

83. J.B. Reducing Corset, faced with
pink silk Milanese. Price 42/– (1925)

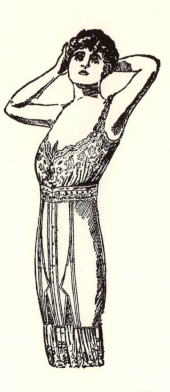

82. C.B. Ultra-fashionable
Model. Price, 7/11
(1915)

84. Harvey Nichols—Brassière,
white, pink or black satin, 39/9.
New porous silk elastic pull-on
belt, 5 guineas (1923)

85 Corselet in pink or white (1927)

but very few women can. Figures are not ageless, more than faces. And yet it is necessary to look un-corseted. The chemise gown, the moyen-âge frock, the draped dress—all the endless variations of the slim and supple silhouette, demand an untrammeled figure. One must yield like the willow—yet how to do that in brocade and steel? Some one has invented a third skin. Corset would be a misnomer. It follows every line of the body, it yields to every motion. The only change it makes in the figure is to mould the flesh to a more beautiful line and hold it firmly in place. The figure is smoothed out, any suggestion of flabbiness is eliminated, and the flesh is held firmly in place beneath the third skin—the elastic girdle. The elastic girdle was not always the unimpeachable garment it is now. It had, like every other innovation, its dark days. Public opinion was against it—and public opinion was more or less justified. The rubber split, the girdle in a short time became loose and shapeless, it was boneless, it rolled down in a hard, ugly constricting wad about the waist; it really was a most unsatisfactory garment. That is all past. The faults of the earlier girdles have all been overcome.   *Harper's Bazaar*

April 1924

During the last two years one very radical change has come about in underclothing. It is the passing of the miscalled camisole, which no longer is an essential part of our wardrobe. With the ever-descending waist-line and a more and more insistent demand for an undisturbed silhouette, it has become apparent that we must at all cost avoid anything likely to emphasise the waist, and that bunchiness or constriction in this region are equally undesirable. It seems a topsy-turvy state of affairs that, though we have never since the days of Ancient Greece been so unrestricted, that never were corsets more important. It also seems rather peculiar that the more exiguous these supports become, the more expensive they usually are. Luckily this is an age of ready-mades, and for all but the woman of very difficult figure, there is generally something to be found at prices ranging from one guinea to three, which will meet the case, and for the really young and slim a sports-belt in elastic, or one of those absurd but attractive little bust bodices all that is required.

The most significant note of fashion in 1924 is the waistline. Venus of Milo would have held up her hands in horror, if she had any, so different is the present standards of beauty. The mere cynic with the humorous outlook has been known to exclaim at the prevailing flatness—hips that passed in the night.

June 1924

Girls who are thin and slightly built need not give much thought as to whether they wear corsets or a belt, for they have little or no superfluous flesh or bulk to keep under; but those who are stoutly built must beware before they cast aside their corset—too much—or they may find their figures suffer in consequence.   *The Queen*

The Crinoline and the Bustle—from Contemporary Magazines

March 1818

Though not in the habit of noticing Court costume, yet as novelty in every way is our object, we cannot refrain from noticing a new court hoop, it is constructed upon a principle which removes all the inconveniences of a hoop; a lady is as much at her ease in one as in her usual dress. They are also smaller than those generally worn and the effect is consequently much more graceful and becoming to the figure.   ACKERMANN'S *Repository of Arts*

September 1832

There is a great tendency to revert to the fashion of hoops, and as an approach to it whalebone is very much employed to give a fullness to the skirt of the dress. A great improvement has been made in the whalebone, it is much more pliant and light than formerly.

September 1833

For making the puckers of dresses full behind, the following simple mode is preferred to any made up "tournures". A piece of starched calico of greater length than width is placed upon a ribbon and falls inside; the ribbon is fastened round the waist, this mode is lighter than any other.

June 1836

We are rapidly approaching the costume represented in the paintings of Watteau and Boucher and in spite of good taste shall shortly arrive at hoops, for the fullness of petticoats increases daily.

April 1839

For supporting the fullness of the skirts of dresses, a moderate description of hoops are worn, they are made of whalebone, having a flexibility which gives grace to the "tournure".

July 1839

The elastic bouffant under petticoats, made of zephyr horse hair, are articles at present very much in request to maintain the fullness of the dresses as substitute for hoops.

September 1839

The horse-hair under petticoats are now almost universally adopted, they are placed underneath the "Gros de Naples" or Cambric petticoat, and serve to give that fullness to the Dress which is now so fashionable, as to be indispensable.

July 1840

Petticoats of "mousseline crinoline" (horse-hair muslin) are usually an accompaniment to the toilettes which leave Paris. For a Ball, they are indispensable to give a rondeur to the figure, and it is acknowledged that the rondeur is at present the perfection of the tournure of an elegant woman.

(Advertisement.) Smith & Lapoulli, St. Paul's Churchyard, have received another large supply of fashionable goods from Paris, comprising every novelty—several boxes of the crino zephyr jupes, demy jupes, and bustles.   *Townsend's Parisian Fashions*

January 1854

In order to give the requisite fullness to the bottom of the dress, straw or a band of crinoline is inserted in the hem, or else the dress is lined—a third, or half-way up the skirt, whichever gives grace to the pleats which would not be clumsy round the waist. These wide skirts should also have sufficient length to hold them out well.

May 1854

This year's most elegant style is the extra fullness at the bottom of the skirt. La mode can make the most exaggerated style attractive and to-day skirts which almost surpass in size the hoops of our ancestors are considered so charming that every method is used to attain the desired volume. For that reason very thin women are wearing crinolines, sometimes even whaleboned petticoats. The method we strongly recommend, which is in the best of taste, and which gives the most grace to the folds of the skirt, is by wearing petticoats of Gros de Tours with deep and very full flounces. The hem has a stiff braid which gives perfect support to the folds of the material. Those who do not like to wear Gros de Tours can have instead starched percale; but then the latter should have two or three deep flounces superimposed one over the other from the hem up to the knee. These flounces give a graceful fall to the pleats of the skirt.

April 1855

In order to attain the enormous circumference which the exaggerated "rondeur" of the dresses demands to-day, petticoats of crinoline (horse-hair) are not enough, some instead are made in piqué with five rows of very thin and supple whalebone, from the hem up to the knees. These petticoats give perfect support but are a little too stiff and bell-like. That is why the elegant woman always prefers petticoats of pou de soie or Gros de Tours, with three fluted flounces, so arranged one over the other as to give the requisite fullness to the bottom of the skirt. Material falls better over these petticoats and they are more gracious in movement. They are worn by women of distinction who understand that charm and elegance come, not from expensive materials and the display of ornament, but from the more intimate refinements of well-cut undergarments.

86 **1875.** Tournure with petticoat which buttons
on to the base of the tournure

87 **1878.** "Plumet" petticoat. The lower flounces
could be removed

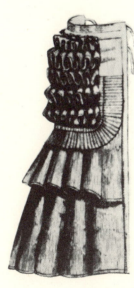

88 **1885.** Horsehair
tournure

89, 90 **1885.** Front and side view of a tournure,
with petticoat attached

BUSTLES OR TOURNURES

91   **1866.** Scarlet drill corsets and a "cage" crinoline
The Gallery of English Costume, Manchester City Art Gallery

June 1856

— By the way, said Mme de D . . . I hope you have not taken to wearing those ridiculous steel and wire petticoats?

— What kind of petticoats?

— Really, my dear, haven't you seen those miracles of progress? Don't you know the latest and most curious fashion? Well, I shall have to tell you all about this pretty bit of frippery. You know the hoops which are used to dry linen?

— Well, what is the connection?

— Just wait! Much more than you would think—That is a petticoat.

— A petticoat? What on earth do you mean?

— Gracious me! Don't you understand—So that a dress should be voluminous and yet have no folds whatever, someone has had the brilliant idea of making underskirts of cane, iron, rubber, and

92. "The Carriage Collapsing Skirt" or "Jupon Passe-Partout", *1865* (from a contemporary advertisement)

finally, the latest creation, a petticoat of circles of steel, like the springs of a watch, and which, held together by bands of elastic, can be folded up and put into one's pocket! The label attached to this article says these petticoats have been patented, but their success remains to be seen.

— How extraordinary! Quite unbelievable.

April 1857

One cannot hope for much modification in the volume of skirts, for the main occupation at the moment is inventing systems whereby the enormous circumference of deep pleats can be supported.

November 1857

It is said that several couturières have decided to curtail a little the size and volume of dresses.—Well, we have our doubts, it is the fashionable woman who accepts or refuses innovations. It is she, and she alone, who has imposed upon us these enormous skirts and she will wear them as long as she pleases. This fashion was born in the highest circles, and the lady of good taste (in spite of what one says), who has increased the size of our dresses is well known. As to the crinoline, the steel cages, etc., they are not worn in those circles. They belong to the common people. Starched petticoats are the only ones admitted in high society; if sometimes a "cage" is worn—from a laudable idea of economy—it is emphatically denied. If skirts diminish this winter it will be because a certain dame à la mode so wished it, and not a certain dressmaker (53).   *Petit Courrier des Dames*

January 1860

Cages are much diminished in circumference; some are almost flat at top, increasing downwards; which imparts a very ungraceful appearance to the figure.   *Le Follet*

September 1860

The iron reign of "Crinoline", as one of our gentlemen wags has called it, is undoubtedly, but gradually, coming to an end. Still, it is reported in the most fashionable Paris journals, that "les jupes se font, toujours aussi amples que par le passé", but at the Sydenham Crystal Palace, where, perhaps, as much of dress in its most fashionable mode can be seen as anywhere in these islands—we noticed some leaders of ton entirely destitute of crinoline. The Parisian ladies are wearing thin dresses, muslin petticoats, with a series of small flounces carried up as far as the waist, each of these flounces being mounted on a piece of steel.

December 1860

Steel petticoats are still universally worn, and are made in various ways—some with cords arranged in points, which are kept at regular distances by the steel, to which each point is fastened, top and bottom; others with the steel fastened in to a coloured material, by means of a runner on the wrong side. Dresses round the bottom of the skirt have rather increased than diminished in size.

May 1862

A great improvement has taken place in the manufacture of "Crinolines"—or, rather, in the make of them—for they are now being arranged with flounces which may be taken off at pleasure. These flounces are buttoned over very few steels, and sometimes are of silk, sometimes of muslin, and sometimes of a thicker material. Crinolines are very much reduced in size at the top, but retain their amplitude at the bottom, and are made with trains to suit the fashionable skirts. The addition of the flounces gives to the dress an elegant and informal appearance, whereas, without them a skirt hangs stiffly and shows where the "cage" commences, which is anything but graceful. Most of the fashionable petticoats are being made with flounces, which assist to throw the dress out at the bottom, and are particularly suitable for wearing under muslin or thin dresses.

August 1867

Crinolines have kept their ground for the summer at least, though much reduced in size. The nicest jupons are those of real crinoline—that is horsehair; it keeps out the dress quite comfortably, without being stiff and unbending like steel circles.

For Crinoline, it is considered quite as inconsistent with the present fashion to be without any as to wear too much of it. A horsehair jupon, however, answers the purpose quite well. It is, of course, much gored, and all underskirts must be gored too.

March 1868

Crinolines, far from being left off, have merely changed their shape; they are plain in front but puffed out on either side so as to remind one strongly of the hoops or paniers of the last century.

November 1868

The pannier tournure is now very generally worn over the crinoline.
                                    Englishwoman's Domestic Magazine

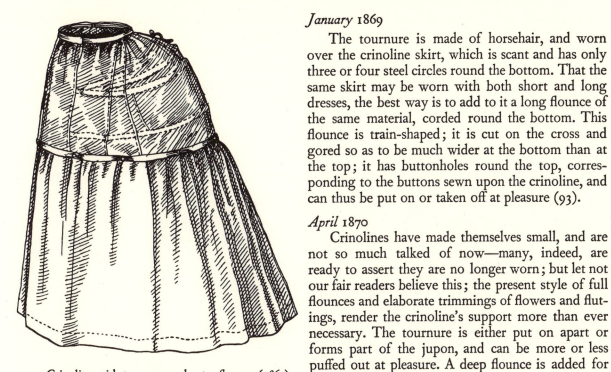

93 Crinoline with tournure and extra flounce (*1869*)

January 1869

The tournure is made of horsehair, and worn over the crinoline skirt, which is scant and has only three or four steel circles round the bottom. That the same skirt may be worn with both short and long dresses, the best way is to add to it a long flounce of the same material, corded round the bottom. This flounce is train-shaped; it is cut on the cross and gored so as to be much wider at the bottom than at the top; it has buttonholes round the top, corresponding to the buttons sewn upon the crinoline, and can thus be put on or taken off at pleasure (93).

April 1870

Crinolines have made themselves small, and are not so much talked of now—many, indeed, are ready to assert they are no longer worn; but let not our fair readers believe this; the present style of full flounces and elaborate trimmings of flowers and flutings, render the crinoline's support more than ever necessary. The tournure is either put on apart or forms part of the jupon, and can be more or less puffed out at pleasure. A deep flounce is added for train-shaped dresses (86).

November 1873

For the rest, the changes are not great—crinoline is no longer worn at all in Paris, but, in spite of many attempts at a plainer style of dress, the tournure still reigns triumphant, and, although less puffed out, still dresses with or without tunics are always more or less draped behind.

Young Englishwoman

April 1873

In Paris no crinoline of any kind is worn excepting the Tournure of fine white horsehair, to keep up the puff in the upper part of the dress. The best model is that which is formed of a number of flutings, put on in hollow pleats, as it keeps up better than anything; there is an elastic strap underneath, to maintain it in the proper place. This tournure should be put on over the under and under the upper skirt worn under the dress, and skirts should be gored in front, and all fullness thrown to the back; a flounce, much deeper at the back than in front, should be added to the upper skirt, especially to wear with a trained dress. These are essential points to a lady who wishes to be *bien juponée* (94, 95).

July 1874

The crinoline lasted a long while, passing through numberless modifications, and was succeeded by the tournure, which has also seen many an alteration in shape, but now the tournure itself is fast disappearing. In several of the most elegant dresses, we have

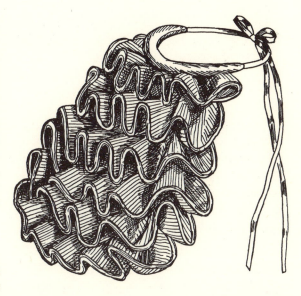

94 Tournure made from six rows of horsehair mounted on a thick calico foundation stiffened with whalebone (*1872*)

123

seen lately, there is no puff whatever, but there are two or three double pleats in the skirt at the back of the waist, giving the required fullness to the train.

Milliner & Dressmaker

January 1876

Flat figures are likely to become as exaggerated as tournures were. The elegantes fasten their skirts to the edge of the corsets.

April 1876

We may remind our readers that the general aspect of la mode has undergone no alterations; skirts are still so tightly strained round the body that all movement is inconvenient and walking almost an impossibility. Bodies are made to fit like wax, with long waists and tight sleeves; all the exaggerations of last year are, in fact still in vogue. A woman must have a remarkably good figure to look well when dressed in this fashion; thin ones look so fragile, that one feels quite sorry for them, and stout ones generally look as if they were suffering agonies. Those who have most wisdom and good taste will endeavour to obey the laws laid down for them to a certain extent, and will carefully avoid all exaggeration.

May 1876

The tournure is much more generally adopted in Paris than here; and in spite of the extreme thinness of the draped figures, the train is bouffant, and the dresses appear to flow over well-shaped tournures. Of these there are several kinds, the short tournure for walking, which is worn low, leaving a flat line from the waist for the cuirasse basque to lie smoothly over. The tournure is so short that it is no inconvenience in sitting down, and is usually worn under walking dresses only. For evening dresses the tournure is longer; the jupon, of which it constitutes a part, is quite plain in front, but at the back flounces, three and five in number, edged with lace or embroidery, which throw out the dress-train. These tournures are also used for carriage costumes. No petticoats but these demi-jupons will be worn throughout the summer under silk dresses. The demi-jupon buttons on to the jupe tournure.

October 1876

There is one detail which it is well to know if one is desirous of following the present fashion, and of wearing the dress as tight as dictated by the latter. Formerly, and not so very long ago either, belted petticoats were worn. At present skirts of this kind are out of fashion; but the corset is furnished with a band of percale closely following the slope of the figure; on this band flat buttons are sewn at regular intervals. These buttons are designed for fastening the buttonholes on the upper edge of the single skirt worn at present. On the under edge of the dress a muslin flounce of prodigious size, trimmed with lace, is sewn; this flounce is longer than the single skirt, which buttons to the corset.

Myra's Journal

1877

Present fashion has set the task of solving the following problem: make a slim dress look rich and elegant, wrap the lady up in a sheath, so that apparently she is deprived of any possibility of movement, while at the same time allow her complete freedom of movement.   *La Mode Illustrée*

September 1878

The mode at the present time threatens us with a complete, or at least a comparative transformation, there being question of replacing the plain fourreau dress with a style partaking at once of the character of the farthingale of the Sixteenth Century, the Marquise panier of the Louis XV period, the crinolines of the Second Empire, and the puffings of the modern costume.   *Myra's Journal*

1879

The fight is on between inflation and flatness. It may last some time but there is no doubt as to the issue. Flatness will succumb. Tournures have already appeared to support the long basques and the large pleats behind. We shall soon hail—perhaps next summer—the restoration of the crinoline, under a new guise perhaps, but doing the same duty.

96 **1884.** A white cotton bustle with an additional "cage", whose size could be regulated by the lacings

The Gallery of English Costume, Manchester City Art Gallery

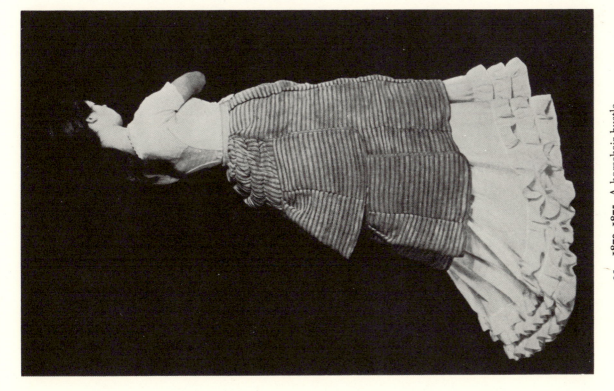

95 **1870–1875.** A horsehair bustle

The Gallery of English Costume, Manchester City Art Gallery

97　*c.* **1800.** "Les Suppléans." "The fashion of false bosoms has at least this utility, that it compels our fashionable fair to wear something"

From a contemporary engraving

1880

There are no more petticoats; there are only "foundation skirts"; on which are constructed the edifice of the top skirt, composed of many bits and pieces; the foundation skirt is plain, shaped exactly like a cotton petticoat. *La Mode Illustrée*

1881

Letters pour in with queries as to the necessity for wearing the tournure, and all kinds of hopes and fears are expressed as to the coming in of crinoline—All fashionable women wear a slight tournure, and even those who long hesitate on the brink of a mode, must own the improvement to most figures.

March 1883

It is curious to note the steady adoption of the tournure. The tournure is stylish if well made and well worn, that is, adapted to the person and the costume. The days are past when one such object could be worn at all times of the day, and the small "puff", which removes the flat look of the matinée differs in construction from the tournure used for walking, or the jupon tournure, which follows its leader in the ball-room. Good taste and much, very much, discretion should be used in selecting a tournure, for it must not only suit the dress but the person wearing it. The small tournure can be fastened by a long stay-hook to the stays, the strings being brought under the front stay-hooks; the long tournure should be made on a jupon, or else sewn into the dress-skirt itself, but it is preferable to wear a properly long jupon-tournure, when used for evening dress, while the short tournure is infinitely preferable for walking (88–90, 96).

September 1884

Exaggeration is to be avoided in all questions of the toilette, but especially as regards the tournure. Always a little absurd, the tournure has reached ridiculous proportions, and from day to day the eye becoming used to the effects has become blinded to the ugly side of a stylish mode. It is not possible for very short ladies to wear as large a tournure as those who are tall, and a too voluminous pouf will destroy the charm of the most elegant toilette.

February 1885

The most notable points with regard to costumes are the gradual diminution in size of the tournure, and the tendency to abandon exaggeratedly long waists. So far from the crinolette becoming fashionable, its first stage, or predecessor, the tournure, is less voluminous, and, as often as not, omitted altogether. A cushion and the drapery of the tunic, with the steels in the skirt, are very often considered sufficient, and give all the effect that is needed.

Myra's Journal

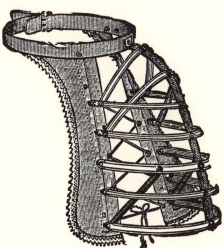

November 1886

Tournures are always worn, even voluminous tournures.

La Mode Illustrée

July 1887

Couturières are doing their best to increase the reasonableness of modern attire by diminishing the size of the tournure; a small cushion fastened on inside the skirt, with a single steel for moderate figures, or two for those that are beyond the medium size, are all that fashion now requires with short dresses. The jupon tournure is still worn with trained dresses, which are apt to fall in at the knees unless supported in some way underneath.

December 1887

In spite of the outcries against the little aids we use to throw the weight of the skirt on the waist—its proper natural support,—

98 "Canfield Bustle"—One of the last bustles to be advertised (*1887*)

a moderate amount of tournure is still worn. In Paris, the modification for the winter season has taken the form of a sharpened outline, narrow, and not unlike a horn in character; far less graceful than is a moderately round tournure.

February 1888

Whatever the style of the dress may be, whether flat or draped, well-dressed women wear scarcely any tournure. The puffed, billowy appearance seen in many evening toilettes is given by the arrangement of the material, and is in no way due to steels, which give an altogether different effect. With corsets made to fit, not to distort the figure, and dresses planned to display the grace of the wearer, and not to alter and travesty all the lines of her contour, we must surely be near the age of reason, which fashion is supposed never to approach!

Myra's Journal

REFERENCES TO CORSETS, CRINOLINES AND BUSTLES FROM CONTEMPORARY SOURCES

1798

Il y a longtemps que la chemise est bannie, car elle ne sert qu'à gâter les contours de la nature; d'ailleurs c'est un attirail incommode et le corset en tricot de soie couleur de chair qui colle sur la taille, ne laisse plus devenir, mais appercevoir tous les charmes secrets. Voilà ce qu'on appelle être vêtue à la sauvage.

Les grande dames commencent à dedaigner les châles dont se parent à leur tour nos sémillantes plébéiennes. Un corset de poupée, étroit et guindé, le remplace et accuse leur taille naguère invisible.

LOUIS-SÉBASTIEN MERCIER, *Tableau de Paris*

1800

Women in general wear stays, very ill-shaped, which by pressing on the back, occasion a roundness of back and shoulders, and impede the free motion of the backs and arms, by forcing them too high, and throwing them back. And this is certainly an absurdity the more provoking as you cannot avoid readily perceiving, that the women's shapes are naturally formed with a capacity of arriving at great ease and elegance; which is evident because they discover a great deal of both under all the disadvantages of this ridiculous fashion . . . I think it necessary to observe, that English women, in general, have not full chests, and that the common sort of people cover the bosoms, as if unwilling to show them. As to such women as have chests well formed, and really handsome, I must remind you of what I have before remarked concerning those abominable stays, which are absolute breast-plates, that destroy this beauty, while they serve the purposes of concealment and defence. How often has virtue been preserved in the world, by its being enabled to resist the first onset! *Lady's Magazine*

1800   *"Dialogue between a Lady and a Man-Milliner"*

— Citizen, I am just come to town, pray have the goodness to inform me how I must appear to be in the fashion?

— Madam, 'tis done in a moment, in two minutes I shall equip you in the first style. Have the goodness to take off that bonnet.

— Well.

— Off that petticoat.

— There it is.

— Away with these pockets.

— There they go.

— Throw off that handkerchief.

— 'Tis done.

— Away with that corset and sleeves.

— Will that do?

— Yes, madame, you are now in the fashion: 'Tis an easy matter you see—to be dressed in the fashion you have only to undress! *Lady's Magazine*

1800   *Edict against the Use of Stays*

The following edict was published throughout the German Empire a few years ago; it seems to prove that one, at least of our fashions originated in Germany:

"Whereas the dangerous consequences arising from the use of stays, are universally acknowledged to impair the health, and impede the growth of the fair sex; when, on the contrary, the suppression of that part of their dress cannot but be effectual in rendering them more fruitful in the marriage state; we hereby strictly enjoin, that in all orphan-houses, nunneries, and other places set apart for the public education of young girls, no stays, of any kind whatever, shall be made use of, or encouraged from henceforth, and from this instant; and it is hereby further noticed to all masters and mistresses of academies and boarding schools, that any girls wearing stays should not be received or countenanced in such schools. We hereby also command, that it be enjoined to the college of physicians that a dissertation, adapted to every one's capacity, be forthwith composed, shewing how materially the growth of children of the female sex is injured by the use of stays, for the better information of parents and school-masters, who wish to procure a handsome shape to their children or pupils, as also those who are not rich enough to alter stays in proportion to the growth of such children or have neglected the means to do it.

The above dissertation shall be distributed gratis, and dispersed among the public; the more so, as whole nations, unacquainted with the use of stays, bring up a race of children remarkable for healthy conditions."

The above Edict was published by the late Emperor, Joseph II.   *Lady's Monthly Museum*

1800–1

But the most uncomfortable style of dress was when they were so scanty that it was difficult to walk in them, and to make them tighter still, invisible petticoats were worn. They were woven in the stocking loom, and were like strait waist-coats, at least as I supposed, but only drawn down over the legs instead of over the arms so that when walking, you were obliged to take short and mincing steps. I was not long in discarding mine and, of course, shocking my juvenile acquaintances by my boldness in throwing off such a fashionable restraint.

The day the eldest daughter was to be presented at Court, we went to see her after she was dressed for the occasion . . . She was, of course, in white silk or satin with pearl ornaments, and a hoop. She was most elegant altogether, but how preposterous her dress would be thought at the present time. Not then to us who had seen so many in that style . . . We used to go to St. James' frequently when Queen Charlotte held a Drawing-room, to see the Ladies. It was very awkward for them when either getting in or out of a carriage as the hoops being too large in circumference, to allow them to pass through the carriage door, without holding the hoop up on one side or down on the other, so that the side they held up showed their little legs and feet which appeared small from the immense rotundity of their dresses, and when they sat in a carriage the hoop came up nearly to their shoulders so that their hands with the fan, could only be seen.   SUSAN SIBBALD, *Memoirs*

1807–10

Hoops were entirely discontinued, except at Court, silk became unfashionable, and printed calicoes and the finest white muslins were substituted, and still hold their influence. The Ladies have, at length, much to their honour, thrown aside those hateful attempts to supply Nature's deficiencies or omissions, the false breasts, pads, and bottoms; and now appear in that native grace and proportion which distinguish the Englishwoman . . . But in the midst of this praise I must be permitted to make one observation: and that is, some thoughtless females indulge in the licence of freedom too far, and shew their persons in a manner offensive to modesty.

J. P. MALCOLM, *Anecdotes of the Manners and Customs of London*

1809

Recéption à l'Hôtel de Ville.—Comme je suffoquais toujours, il m'arracha mes colliers, déchira ma robe, mon corset, brisa tous les cordons, les lacets, et, grâce à ces soins d'un veritable intérêt, je respirai.

DUCHESSE D'ABRANTÈS, *Mémoires*

100 **1804.** "Corset Élastique." The possibilities of rubber in the form of elastic as a corset material were early recognised, but more than a hundred years were to pass before corsets made entirely from elastic came into general wear

99 **1806.** "The Marchioness of Townshend in her full Court dress, as worn by her Ladyship on the Queen's Birthday." The large panier was still *obligatoire* for Court, although the fashionable waist was very high

Both from contemporary prints

Progress of the Toilet. — THE STAYS. — Plate 1.

101   **1810.** A transitional corset: note the gusset on the hips, the top of the corset slit to allow for a rounder bust, and also the heavy busk which is still retained

From a caricature by James Gillray

1810

Stays are now composed, not of whalebone, indeed, or hardened leather, but of bars of iron and steel from three to four inches broad, and many of them not less than eighteen in length . . . It is by no means uncommon to see a mother lay her daughter down upon the carpet, and placing her foot on her back, break half-a-dozen laces in tightening her stays.

Quoted in *The Corset and the Crinoline*

1811

When the arts of sculpture and painting, in their fine specimens from the chisels of Greece and the pencils of Italy, were brought into this country, taste began to mould the dress of our female youth after their more graceful fashion. The health-destroying bodice was laid aside; brocades and whalebone disappeared; and the easy shape and flowing drapery again resumed the rights of nature and of grace.

Thus, for a short time, did the Graces indeed preside at the toilet of British beauty. But a strange caprice seems now to have dislodged these gentle handmaids. We see immodesty on one side, unveiling the too redundant bosom; on the other, deformity, once more drawing the steeled bodice upon the bruised ribs.

But, though the hoop and quilted petticoat are no longer suffered to shroud in hideous obscurity one of the loveliest works of nature, yet all intermediate covering is not to be banished. Modesty, on one hand, and Health on the other, still maintain the law of "fold on fold".

Some of our fair dames appear, summer and winter, with no other shelter from sun or frost, than one single garment of muslin or silk over their chemise—if they wear one! but that is often dubious. The indelicacy of this mode need not be pointed out; and yet, O shame it is most generally followed.

The Mirror of the Graces

c. 1814

I was for several days much alarmed by a change that I saw in the shape of the Princess's figure (Princess Caroline of Wales), and I could not help imparting the terrible fear I felt to Lady ———. She also had noticed it; but I was much relieved by her telling me she knew for certain it was only caused by the Princess having left off stays—a custom which she is very fond of. She ought to be warned not to indulge in this practice; for it might give rise to reports exceedingly injurious to her character.

The quantity of rouge the Parisian Ladies wear, is to an English eye very disagreeable. The tournure of their throat and person, is with few exceptions, extremely elegant, and said to be greatly improved since the revolution by the disuse of stays, and other contrivances which have succeeded them.

LADY CHARLOTTE BURY, *Diary of a Lady in Waiting*

c. 1820

"*On Fashion.*"—Our belles formerly overloaded themselves with dress, of late years they have affected to go about almost naked—"and are, when unadorned, adorned the most". The women have left off stays, the men have taken to wear them.   WILLIAM HAZLITT, *The Plain Speaker*

1820

"*Modern Male Fashions*"

Faces painted deepest brown,
 Waistcoats strip'd and gaudy,
Sleeves, thrice doubled, thick with down,
 And stays, to brace the body!

"*Modern Female Fashions*"

Red elbows, thin gauze sleeves, that add
 An icy covering merely;
A wadded corset, Nelson pad;
 Like Dutch women—or nearly.

La Belle Assemblée

133

1820

Fanny and I went to Court; the Drawing-room was very full, but as hoops are abolished it was much pleasanter and less fatiguing . . . The costumes were all the same as the French Court and I think very pretty.
HON. MRS. CALVERT, *An Irish Beauty of the Regency*

1837

When the young lady spends a quarter of an hour in lacing her stays as tight as possible, and is sometimes seen by her female friends pulling hard for some minutes, next pausing to breathe, then resuming the task with might and main, till after perhaps a third effort she at last succeeds and sits down covered with perspiration, then it is that the effect of stays is not only injurious to the shape but is calculated to produce the most serious consequences.
MRS. WALKER, *Female Beauty*

1834

The diameter of the fashionable ladies at present is about three yards; their bustles (false bottoms) are the size of an ordinary sheep's fleece. The very servant girls wear bustles! Eliza Miles told me a maid of theirs went out one Sunday with three kitchen dusters pinned on as a substitute.

1844

Mrs. Ame's musical soirée—Most of the men were Unitarians the men with faces like a meat-axe, the women most palpably without bustles,—a more unloveable set of human beings I never looked on.
MRS. J. W. CARLYLE, *Letters*

1840's

Mlle. Mars.—Her features did not bear any trace of past beauty, and her figure had lost all the slightness of youth. The process of dressing her up for the stage was a long and painful one, and was said to have been done by degrees, beginning at early dawn; the tightening being gradually intensified until the stage hour, when it has been rumoured that the finale was accomplished by the maid's foot being placed in the small of the lady's back, and that thus the last vigorous haul was given to the refractory stay lace.
CAPTAIN GRONOW, *Reminiscences and Recollections*

1850's

La crinoline, cette étoffe d'un tissu raide, comme fabriqué avec du fil d'archal, s'était unie à une autre invention de jupons à jour formant à l'œil comme une cage à poulet. Ces deux combinations réunies servent à faire ballonner les robes pour leur donner l'ampleur à la mode, grâce à laquelle les femmes ressemblent à une cloche. Les uns disent que c'est hideux, d'autres que c'est cossu. L'œil s'y est habitué, et l'œil est le grand maître de la mode puisque c'est pour lui qu'on l'invente.

L'Empereur et l'Imperatrice arrivés, on a passé dans la salle de théâtre ou l'on a eu toutes les peines du monde à se caser, les crinolines prenant toute la place. Les messieurs ont erré comme des âmes en peine, maugréant contre l'ampleur de la mode qui les reléguait dans les pièces voisines.
COMTESSE TASCHER DE LA PAGERIE, *Mon Séjour aux Tuileries*

1850's

At the commencement of the Empire the fashion was very peculiar. Modern ladies of fashion who dress their slim bodies with skirts narrowly draped would tremble with horror if they had to appear in such finery as was then in vogue, and which was supported by a kind of frame with pliable steel springs, the size of which would scarcely admit of three women to be seated or to stand in a boudoir of a small house at the same time . . .

Female skill would indeed have had to be great in order to devise any advantage from such peculiar fashions. To walk with so immense a paraphernalia around one was not very easy; and the slender body, placed in the centre of this volume of material, appeared to be detached from the rest of the body altogether. To be able to sit so as not to cause the rebellious springs to fly open, required a miracle of precision. To get into a carriage without rumpling the delicate fabrics—for evening toilettes were made of tulle and lace—required a great deal of time, much quietness on the part of the horses and much patience on the part of the fathers and husbands, whose complaisance was put to an enormous test, compelled as they were to remain motionless in the midst of these 'images fragiles'.

Among other problems to be solved were: How to travel? How to lie down? How to rock a cradle? And even how to hold hands when out for a walk? About this period the offering of one's arm to a lady, either in the salons or when accompanying her in the street, was quite out of fashion . . .

This style tyrannised over a whole generation until at last the ladies found a deliverer in Worth, who introduced the crinoline; and, since then, every lady and every peasant woman alike, has offered this worthy man her tribute. We owe to the artistic taste of this great milliner, and to his intuition for aesthetic elegance, the revival of grace in dress. He modified the volume of the skirts, roughly at first, it is true—for the body so as to allow it greater freedom; and, when in 1864 I arrived at the Court, scarcely any hoops were worn, whilst the round and narrow skirts permitted one to go out without causing any obstruction in the streets or catastrophes in the apartments.

MME CARETTE, *My Mistress, the Empress Eugènie*

1856

Fanny was struck with a new idea. "Please, ma'am, my sister-in-law has got an aunt as lives Lady's maid with Sir John's daughter—Miss Arley. And they did say as she wore iron petticoats all made of hoops——" "Nonsense, Fanny!" we all cried; for such a thing had not been heard of in all Drumble, let alone Cranford, and I was rather looked upon in the light of a fast young woman by all the laundresses of Cranford because I had two corded petticoats . . .

"I have wondered how I could best fulfil your commission to me to purchase something fashionable and pretty for dear Miss Pole, and at length I have decided upon one of the new kind of "cages", which are made so much lighter and more elegant in Paris than in England. Indeed, I am not sure if they have ever reached you, for it is not a month since I saw the first of the kind in Paris." (106)

MRS. GASKELL, *The Cage at Cranford*

1856

"*Crinolineomania.*" Crinolineomania may be said to be essentially a female complaint, although many of the other sex—husbands in particular—are continually complaining of it . . . That Crinolineomania is of foreign origin Dr. Punch considers there is little room for doubt; indeed, if he were called upon to fix the spot precisely where the malady broke out, without hesitation he would point to Paris. Dr. Punch has ample grounds for his belief that the persons first affected were the ladies attached to the Imperial Court; and it is a more than mere surmise with him, that symptoms of the mania were primarily betrayed by the young and lovely Empress.

1857

"*Crinoline Viewed as a Depopulating Influence.*" Among the causes which are cited to account for the decreasing rate of increase of the French population, it is thought that the spread of the Crinoline contagion is proving most injurious in its effects upon the census. The mode now prevailing is one of such extravagance that it is continually

102 The first appearance of "Crinoline" in *Punch* (*August 1856*)

135

demanding fresh sacrifices, and ladies have to choose between a fine dress and a family, for no income but a Rothschild's can provide for both.

1857

"*How About the Hoops?*" "Wide skirts still continue to be worn, and there is but little apprehension of their going out: it having been decided that the mode is most becoming." Now, ladies, by whom, do you imagine this decision has been come to ? . . . Your object in dress, we presume, is to please; and not to please yourselves so much as male admirers. Now you don't suppose hoop petticoats are looked upon with favour by the masculine eye-sight? You surely can't imagine there is "metal more attractive" to a man in half a ton of Crinoline than in nature's flesh and blood unsurrounded by steel armour? If you wish to dissipate such fond delusion, empanel a jury of your nearest male relations, whom gallantry will not deter from giving a true verdict. Or even put the question to your partner in a ball-room, and see if he approves of the fashion which makes ladies unapproachable. Whether as a waltzer or as husband, a man likes a woman he can take to his arms; and how is this possible when she is entrenched in an impregnable hoop petticoat, which when he approaches he breaks his shin against?

1858

"*Place aux Dames!*" Wherever hoops do congregate, there must be room to trundle them. While ladies raise such structures round themselves as they are doing, the dimensions of these structures must be architecturally considered. Staircases must be widened, and porticos enlarged, and seats be set apart much farther than they used to be. In short, in all their measurements builders must leave ample margin for the petticoats, and be careful that the air-tubes be allowed sufficient area. It is a new thing to us to say anything in favour of the Crinoline monstrosities, but we must admit that the present width of fashion, may, masculinely viewed, be found of some advantage. For instance, thanks to large and lovely woman, Covent Garden is so built that a man may stretch his legs in it. No Paterfamilias can any more deny his wife and daughters the favour of his escort, on the ground that he will be tortured by the closeness of the seats. The house has been constructed to accommodate the higher and wider classes, we gentlemen of England may loll there at our ease, and sit through a whole opera uncramped as to our knees, etc. Decidedly, for this we have to thank the ladies.

1862

"*The Despotism of Dress.*" Not all the powers of ridicule, nor the remonstrances of affection have been able to beat down that inflated absurdity, called Crinoline! It is a living institution, which nothing seemingly can crush or compress.

1865

"*Ladies and Their Long Tails.*" Crinoline at length is going out, thank goodness! In matters of costume, lovely woman rarely ceases to make herself a nuisance; and the length of her skirt now is almost as annoying as, a while ago, its width was.

1858   "*Aphorisms upon Tight-Lacing*"

A narrowness of waist betrays a narrowness of mind. When the ribs are contracted, it is a sure sign that the intellect is also.

Better to have good lungs and what, in the wisdom of "Le Follet" is considered a bad figure, than by a tight corset to get a better shape and a worse constitution.

When a pair of stays comes in at the door, health, paired with happiness, flies out of the window.

She, who, from tight-lacing, cannot draw a long breath, will probably in no long time have no breath at all to draw.

What's bred in the whalebone will eventually "come out" in the visits to the doctor.

Give me the unmaking of a lady's stays, and I care not who makes up her dresses.   *Punch*

Would bee's for 1819—or DANDYZETTE'S TOILETTE.
pub. by Mr Cleary. 39. Nassau St Dublin.

103   **1819.** A small pad was worn at the back throughout the "classical" period, but it increased in size as the skirts themselves grew wider and became the "bustle" of the eighteen-thirties

From a contemporary print

105   1830. "La Marchande de Corsets." The beginning of the nineteenth-century corset, showing the rounder curves given by the insertion of gussets

104   1805. "The Looking Glass in Disgrace." The last version of the eighteenth-century stays, short and lightly boned

Both from contemporary prints

1858

Les femmes ont raison, qui maintiennent la crinoline malgré les plaisanteries, les caricatures, les vaudevilles et les avanies de toute sorte. Elles font bien de préférer ces jupes amples, étoffées, puissantes, largement étalées à l'œil, aux étroits fourreaux où s'engainaient leurs grand-mères et leurs mères. De cette abondance de plis, qui vont s'évasant comme la fustanelle d'un derviche tourneur, la taille sort élégante et mince; le haut du corps se détache avantageusement, toute la personne pyramide d'une manière gracieuse. Cette masse de riches étoffes fait comme un piédestal au buste et à la tête, seules parties importantes maintenant que la nudité n'est plus admise. Une jeune femme décolletée, les bras découverts, traînant après elle des flots de moire antique, de satin ou de taffetas, avec ses doubles jupes ou ses volants multiples, nous semble aussi belle et aussi bien costumée que possible, et nous ne voyons pas trop ce que l'art aurait à lui reprocher.

THÉOPHILE GAUTIER, *De la Mode*

c. 1860

Au Pensionnat. — Bien qu'elle fût considerée comme absolument indépendante, Jenny n'osait pas mettre la "cage" formellement interdite par le règlement. Elle la remplaçait par des jupons amidonnés qui soulevaient joliment sa jupe et faisaient, dès qu'elle remuait, un bruissement joyeux. — Tu nous trouves miteuses, hein? — Avec nos robes qui plaquent, nous avons l'air de parapluies mal fermés . . .

— Oh! pas du tout — Je me disais, au contraire, que vous avez de bien plus jolies tournures que les dames de Nancy. Les "cages", c'est hideux! Clothilde me regarde avec étonnement. A ce moment-là, aucune femme n'admettait la possibilité de s'habiller sans cage. Elle dit:

— Tu bafouilles — C'est très jolie — Mais ici, y a pas de mèche! Jenny, elle, met des jupons empesés, alors elle est présentable.

1861

Longchamps. Un grand brouhaha se produit. C'est un prix important qui va être couru. Les femmes grimpent sur des chaises. C'est un océan de cages qui se balancent, montrant des jambes, qui me semblent courtes et lourdes pour la plupart. Que les tailles de ce temps-là fussent en général sans grâce, trop minces entre des poitrines trop rebondies et des hanches trop étoffées, cela s'explique par la déformation du corset qui les faisait telles que les voulait la mode . . . Quand la course toucha à sa fin, toutes les femmes se penchèrent brusquement en avant, et la pression des cages contre les chaises les fit se redresser en arrière en éventail. Alors, on aperçut jusqu'à la taille des dessous qui ne se ressemblaient pas comme les jambes . . . Il faisait très chaud et la plupart des femmes n'avaient pas mis de "petit jupon", c'est-à-dire de jupon entre le pantalon et la cage. Et j'aperçus, à ma grande surprise, ce que je n'avais vu encore: des petits lambeaux d'étoffe qui pendaient ridicules et pitoyables. Je tirai mon oncle par sa manche et je lui montrai les objets de mon étonnement.

— Qu'est-ce que c'est qu'ça? . . .

— Ça — dit l'oncle de sa voix un peu discordante . . . c'est les chemises qui sortent des pantalons ouverts. . . .

Je répétai, ahurie de plus en plus:

— Des pantalons ouverts. . . . Alors à quoi bon un pantalon s'il est ouvert?

En entendant la reponse bruyante de l'Oncle, plusieurs femmes étaient descendues précipitamment de leurs chaises. Je ne dis pas "avaient sauté", car, avec les corsets durs, à longs buscs, les mouvements manquaient plutôt de souplesse et de rapidité.

GYP, *Souvenirs d'une Petite Fille*

C'était la seule fois que j'ai vu l'Impératrice en costume de cour, et c'était vraiment une admirable vision. Elle semblait grande malgré l'horrible "cage" qui l'élargissait et diminuait à l'œil sa hauteur.

En 1870, on avait, depuis cinq ans au moins, abandonné les horribles "cages", mais on portait encore des jupons "amidonnés".

GYP, *Du Temps des Cheveux et des Chevaux*

1864

When the rooms are done, pray charge the maids not to rub on the clean paper with their abominably large crinolines.

I went yesterday to have a dress fitted at Elsie's . . . Elsie was disengaged and came to the fitting room herself and she would not let me have the thing done anyhow, as I wanted, saying to her French Dressmaker: "Because Madame will not wear a crinoline and will not be tied up, that is no reason why she should have no waist and no style."
                                                                MRS. J. W. CARLYLE, *Letters*

1865

"Rhymes to Decreasing Crinoline"

With exceeding satisfaction
A remarkable contraction
Of thy petticoat our eyes have lately seen;
The expanse of ladies' dress,
Thank its yielding arbitress,
Growing beautifully less,
                    Crinoline

On the flagstones of the street
If a man two women meet,
He may pass, if pretty tolerably lean,
And sufficiently alert,
Stepping not into the dirt
'Twixt the kennel and thy skirt,
                    Crinoline

Now when ladies go to Court,
Let us hope that no more sport
They will furnish to the rabble vile and mean,
While their clothes, for want of room,
Stick right out of every brougham;
For retrenchment is thy doom,
                    Crinoline

There will soon be room for us
In the public omnibus,
When the middle class of ladies find the Queen,
And the fair Princess of Wales,
And Nobility's females,
Have all had to reef their sails,
                    Crinoline

When to church young damsels go,
Their habiliments to show,
In their bonnets of magenta, mauve and green,
A not very spacious pew
Will suffice to hold a few,
If the darlings but eschew
                    Crinoline

No more ladies death will find,
In their frames of steel calcined,
Set on blazes by a grate without a screen;
Though some cookmaids yet may flare,
Who dress out, and don't take care,
For the servants still will wear,
                    Crinoline

But the dashing stylish belles,
And the exquisite fast swells,
Will deride the grotesque fashion that has been
For so long a time the rage
In a comical past age;
Thy preposterous old cage,
                    Crinoline.

1865

"*Philosophy of Fashion.*" When hoops went out of vogue nigh on a century ago, the ladies vowed that scanty petticoats were infinitely prettier; and they vied with one another in reducing their dimensions, until their skirts became so shrunken they could hardly move their feet with the limited circumference. So doubtless, will it be again, now Crinoline is doomed. The milliners of Paris have determined on reviving the "costume of the Empire" of some fifty seasons since, and who will dare dispute the mandates of the milliner. Already we see signs of the change which is approaching. Ladies fresh from Paris startle our eyes now-a-days by appearing in what at first sight we might fancy are their night-dresses. Of course, when once the tide sets in, all the female world will swim with it. Casting overboard their Crinoline, the Ladies will all look as though they had been put under a rigid course of Banting. Our wives will be so altered that we shall hardly know them; and, when they walk out in their limp and scanty dresses, we shall at first be scarcely able to realise our happiness in missing the accustomed chaffing of our shins. *Punch*

1867

Correspondence. I was placed at the age of fifteen at a fashionable school in London, and there it was the custom for the waists of the pupils to be reduced one inch per month until they were what the lady principal considered small enough. When I left school at seventeen, my waist measured only thirteen inches, it having been formerly twenty-three inches in circumference. Every morning one of the maids used to come to assist us to dress, and a governess superintended, to see that our corsets were drawn as tight as possible. After the first few minutes every morning I felt no pain, and the only ill effects apparently were occasional headaches and loss of appetite. I should be glad if you will inform me if it is possible for girls to have a waist of fashionable size and yet preserve their health. Very few of my fellow pupils appeared to suffer, except the pain caused by the extreme tightness of the stays. In one case where the girl was stout and largely built, two strong maids were obliged to use their utmost force to make her waist the size ordered by the lady principal—viz., seventeen inches; and though she fainted twice while the stays were being made to meet, she wore them without seeming injury to her health, and before she left school she had a waist measuring only fourteen inches, yet she never suffered a day's illness. Generally all the blame is laid by parents on the principal of the school, but it is often a subject of the greatest rivalry among the girls to see which can get the smallest waist, and often while the servant was drawing in the waist of my friend to the utmost of her strength, the young lady, though being tightened till she had hardly breath to speak, would urge the maid to pull the stays yet closer, and tell her not to let the lace slip in the least. I think this is a subject which is not sufficiently understood. Though I have always heard tight-lacing condemned, I have never suffered any ill effects myself, and, as a rule, our school was singularly free from illness.

1868

Quotation from the "Lancet". Our attention has been directed to a recent number of a popular journal, in which the advocates for Tight-lacing ventilate their erroneous views. It is certainly much to be regretted that any Englishwoman should torture herself or her children by employing tight or unyielding stays or belts. The mischief produced by such a practice can hardly be overestimated. It tends gradually to displace the most important organs of the body, while, by compressing them, it must from the first interfere with their functions. The grounds upon which Tight-lacing has been recommended are diametrically opposed to the teachings of anatomy and physiology, not to say common sense.

1869

"To the Slaves of Fashion"

You must try and lace me tighter, lace me tighter, mother dear;
My waist, you know, is nearly half the size it was last year;
I will not faint again, mother, I care not what they say,
Oh! It's sixteen inches today, mother, it's sixteen inches today.

There's many a wee, wee waist they say, but none so wee as mine;
I'm five-foot-five-and-a-half in height, my inches forty-nine;
Last year my waist was—Oh! It's size I'd be afraid to say,
But it's sixteen inches today, mother, it's sixteen inches today.

You must lace me tight tonight, mother, I must try and keep this size,
I know the doctors tell you it is dangerous—unwise,
And they call me vain and foolish, but I care not what they say,
For it's sixteen inches today, mother, its sixteen inches today.

I stay so quiet all day, mother, afraid the cords might burst,
I can breathe quite freely now, though it hurt me so at first;
At first it hurt me very much, but now I'm happy and gay
For it's sixteen inches today, mother, it's sixteen inches today.

You remember the first month, mother, what agony I bore,
But I went through it without flinching; the corsets that I wore
Measured seven-and-twenty inches; Oh I care not what they say,
For it's sixteen inches today, mother, it's sixteen inches today.

1869

"The Lay of the Lacer"

Don't lace me tighter, sister dear;
   I never had supposed,
That it would give me so much pain
   "My dear, they're not near closed."
Then I must get a larger pair
   To clasp my clumsy waist,
Of this I'm sure, I cannot bear
   To feel myself tight-laced.
Oh, the misery of tight-lacing
   None but have tried can tell;
I'm sure that as to figure,
   I cannot be a belle.
The pain, say you, it will not last?
   Well! I will try again;
Lace me up tightly, sister dear,
   I'll try and bear the pain.

106 *c.* **1856.** The steel-frame crinoline appeared in 1856; from its construction it was often referred to as a "cage"

From a contemporary print

107 **c. 1858.** "The Picnic." "Among other problems to be solved was: How to lie down?" Obviously these young ladies are not wearing the patent collapsing crinoline, in which, as the advertisement says, "the most unwary or careless sitter is spared the mortification entailed should her crinoline fly up."

From a contemporary print

Do lace me tighter, sister dear,
  I never had supposed
It would give me so much pleasure.
  "My dear, the corset's closed."
Then I must get a smaller pair
  To clasp my slender waist;
Full well you know I cannot bear,
  To feel I'm not tight-laced.
Oh, the pleasure of tight-lacing,
  I that have tried, can tell;
Besides that, as to the figure,
  I feel I'm quite a belle.
This is the teaching of my lay,
  Lace tightly while you can;
Be sure you'll soon forget the pain
  You feel when you began.

Englishwoman's Domestic Magazine

1877

"Bosom Secrets."—When a lady of Mr. Punch's acquaintance was in Paris not very long ago, she ordered a dress at a famous Modiste's but found, when she tried it on that she could hardly breathe. On her complaining to the Modiste that the dress was too tight over the chest, "Que voulez-vous, Madame?" exclaimed the faithful follower—if not framer—of the fashion. "On ne porte plus de gorge." (Bosoms are not worn now.) "Qu'est-ce qu'on fait donc?" asked her innocent English customer. "Mais, Madame, on ôte la ouate." (Oh, they take out the wadding) was the equally innocent answer. Punch had never fully appreciated the bearings of this perfectly true story till the other day when he came upon the following paragraph in one of the leading ladies' journals: "Buy a pair of Maintenon corsets, fitting your waist measure. The other parts of the corset will be proportioned as you ought to be. Put the corset on, and fill the vacant spaces with fine jewellers' wool, then tack on a piece of soft silk or cambric over the bust thus formed to keep the wool in place, renewing it as often as required. This is the most natural and effectual mode of improving the figure which I have heard of." Now Punch sees how exactly the Parisian Modiste's plan came home to her own business and her customers' bosoms.

1876

"Lines Picked up at the Brixton Rink"

Upon the Rink the Lady sat,
Beside her lay her dainty hat,
  All crumpled;
She looked the picture of distress,
So dusty was her pretty dress,
  And rumpled!
"I can't get up," in faltering tone,
She said. I thought that, perhaps alone
  She could not.
I picked her up. She was not hurt
'Twas but the tightness of her skirt—
  She could not!

Punch

1880

"*Fashionable Clothing.*" One sees, with a feeling of profoundest pity, the waists which otherwise well-grown young women are not ashamed to exhibit in public places, to the amazement of all who know what the compression has been by which they were produced. Waists which ought to be 25 or 26 inches in circumference are reduced to 19; and when sensible dressmakers object (as sometimes is

done), the answer is given, "Oh, you make the waist of so many inches, and I'll engage to get into it."
How the "getting into it" is effected, is one of the "secrets of the prison house", which we are glad
not to be called upon to divulge. But we do not wonder at nervous headaches, feelings of "sinking"
which call for strong tea or coffee, or sherry; back aches and pains in the sides, indigestion and poor
appetite, short breath and imperfect circulation, cold hands and feet (and even red noses), not to speak
of other maladies, of a less directly evident, a more painful and more deadly kind. One does not wonder at the sharp tempers of the young ladies with the wasp waists: but one is glad one is not obliged
to associate with them.   *The Queen*

1881   "*The Chant of the Crinolette*"

> " Tell me not in honeyed accents Crinoline will come once more,
> That my soul must feel the trammels that I felt in days of yore;
> Modesty, I own, forbids me to the public to reveal
> All the tortures that I suffered in the period of steel;
> Philistine I was then, doubtless, and those days would fain forget,
> Why revive the old wire-fencing, though you call it Crinolette?
>
> Who's responsible, I ask you, for this strange portentous birth
> Of an ancient hideous fashion, and an echo answers "Worth" . . .
> Then again, at Fashion's dictates we must give up fringe of hair,
> Which aesthetic folks have stated is the thing we ought to wear . . .
> We'll not yield without a struggle, so, fair Ladies, do not fret—
> Stick to Fourteenth-century fringes, and abjure the Crinolette."

                                                                                          Punch

End of the Nineteenth Century

The thought of the discomfort, restraint and pain, which we had to endure from our clothes, makes
me even angrier now than it did then; for in those days nearly everyone accepted their inconveniences
as inevitable. Except for the most small-waisted, naturally dumb-bell-shaped females, the ladies never
seemed at ease, or even quite as if they were wearing their own clothes. For their dresses were always
made too tight, and the bodices wrinkled laterally from the strain; and the stays showed in a sharp
ledge across the middles of their backs. And in spite of whalebone, they were apt to bulge below the
waist in front; for, poor dears, they were but human after all, and they had to expand somewhere.
How my heart went out to a fat French lady we met once in a train, who said she was going into the
country for a holiday 'pour prendre mes aises sans corset'. . . . We did rebel against stays. Margaret
says that the first time she was put into them—when she was about thirteen—she ran round and
round the nursery screaming with rage. I did not do that. I simply went and took them off; endured
sullenly the row which ensued, when my soft-shelled condition was discovered; was forcibly re-
corseted; and, as soon as possible went away and took them off again. . . . I had a bad figure, and to
me they were real instruments of torture; they prevented me from breathing, and dug deep holes into
my softer parts on every side, I am sure no hair-shirt could have been worse to me . . .

Once I asked Aunt Etty what it had been like to wear a crinoline. "Oh it was delightful!" she said.
"I've never been so comfortable since they went out. It kept your petticoats away from your legs and
made walking so light and easy."   GWEN RAVERAT, *Period Piece*

End of the Nineteenth and Beginning of the Twentieth Centuries

Et puis j'ai vu les tournures, et je pourrais dire comme François Coppée : — "et je n'ai pas trouvé cela
si ridicule." Les femmes ne peuvent-elles pas tout porter, et n'ont-elles pas le secret de rendre beau,
ou de faire admettre l'invraisemblable et l'outre-cuidant? Ces parures, qu'on appelait des strapontins,
étaient recouvertes d'un amas d'étoffes drapées, travaillées, coulissées avec art par les grands faiseurs
d'alors, et paraissaient légères malgré leur abondance. . . .

Je me mis au travail avec plus d'ardeur que jamais, stimulé par la faveur de M. Doucet. Je composai toute une collection de costumes, qui comportaient des jaquettes et des jupes serrées à la taille. Les femmes les portaient sur des corsets, qui étaient de véritables gaines, des armatures, dans lesquelles elles étaient incarcerées depuis la gorge jusqu'aux genoux; la jupe devait former par terre un certain nombre de godets. . . .

C'était encore l'époque du corset. Je lui livrai la guerre. La dernier représentant de ces appareils maudits s'appelait le Gache Sarraute. Certes, j'ai toujours connu les femmes encombrées de leurs avantages et soucieuses de les dissimuler ou de les répartir. Mais ce corset les classait en deux massifs distincts; d'un côté, le buste, la gorge, les seins, de l'autre, le train de derrière tout entier, de sorte que les femmes, divisées en deux lobes, avaient l'air de tirer une remorque. C'était presque un retour à la tournure. Comme toutes les grandes révolutions, celle-là s'était faite au nom de la Liberté, pour donner libre cours au jeu de l'estomac, qui pouvait se dilater sans mesure. Il occupait le dessous du lobe supérieur.

C'est encore au nom de la Liberté que je préconisai la chute du corset et l'adoption du soutien-gorge qui, depuis a fait fortune. Oui, je libérais le buste, mais j'entravais les jambes. On se souvient des pleurs, des cris, des grincements de dents, que causa cet ukase de la mode. Les femmes se plaignaient de ne plus pouvoir marcher, ni monter en voiture. Toutes leurs jérémiades plaidaient en faveur de mon innovation. Est-ce qu'on écoute encore leurs protestations? N'ont-elles pas poussé les mêmes gémissements quand elles sont revenues à l'ampleur? Leurs plaintes ou leurs bougonnements ont-ils jamais arrêté le mouvement de la mode, ou en ont-ils au contraire favorisé la publicité? Tout le monde porta la jupe étroite. . . .

Quand j'ai annoncé la disparation du corset, même sensation. Tous les Présidents des Chambres Syndicales intéressées me représentaient que je mettais à pied toute une fourmilière d'ouvrières. Il fallut leur expliquer que les femmes et leurs corsets s'étaient toujours transformés dans l'histoire, et qu'elles se transformeraient encore. Ils devaient se tenir prêts à toute eventualité.

PAUL POIRET, *En Habillant L'Epoque*

c. 1910

Le théâtre lui-même en voyait de dures avec la mode, par ce temps de grands corsets qui soulevaient la gorge vers le haut, abattaient la croupe, creusaient le ventre. Germaine Gallois, inflexible beauté bastionnée, n'acceptait pas de rôles "assis". Gainée d'un corset qui commençait sous l'aisselle et finissait près des genoux, deux ressorts de fers plats dans le dos, deux autres au long des hanches, une "tirette" d'entre-jambes (j'emploie les mots de l'époque) maintenant l'édifice dont le laçage en outre exigeait un lacet de six metres, elle restait debout, entr-actes compris, de huit heures trente à minuit. . . .

COLETTE, *Mes Apprentissages*

1920's

Court, plat, géométrique, quadrangulaire, le vêtement feminin s'établit sur des gabarits qui dépendent du parallélogramme, et 1925 ne saluera pas le retour de la mode à courbes suaves, du sein arrogant, de la savoureuse hanche.　　COLETTE, quoted by LIBRON ET CLOUZET, *Le Corset dans l'Art*

APPENDIX I

The Construction of Corsets

CORSETRY is a highly specialised branch of dressmaking; the designing, cutting, and fitting is usually done by men and the execution by expert needlewomen, or rather in this present day by expert machinists.

An exact reproduction of period corsets would require considerable skill and many hours of work; they can, however, be very much simplified if required for any modern use, provided the correct cut and main boning are retained. The amount of finish depends on whether they are to be worn under a dress to give the right silhouette or worn to be seen, and also the length of time they are to be worn.

Several contemporary texts are quoted in the following instructions as, apart from their interest, it is always easier to simplify if the original method of construction is understood.

Patterns

The separate pattern pieces are arranged on the page in the order in which they are joined together.

Extra gussets or basques are lettered to show where they should be inserted.

The pieces are laid as they should be cut from the material; that is, the straight edges of the page represent the warp and weft weaves.

The scale in inches is given on each pattern.

Corsets should be cut two inches smaller than actual bust and waist measurements to allow for tight lacing; they should never quite meet when laced.

Sixteenth-, Seventeenth-, and Eighteenth-century Corsets

The patterns given are all wearable by a modern woman; the only point which presents any difficulties is her present breadth of shoulder. This, however, is easily rectified by adding to the centre back of the pattern. This difference is not surprising when it is remembered that children were put into corsets as soon as they could walk; the shoulder blades were thus permanently pulled back to give the fashionable narrow straight back, and a consequent greater development of chest and bust occurred.

These stays do not unduly compress the waist, but they have other points of discomfort. As emphasis is on length of body they press down on to the hips and reach high up under the armpits; also the tight shoulder-straps cut across the top of the arm or shoulder. Many original stays will be found with pieces of chamois leather round the armholes and lining the tabs from the waist.

149

If the correct stays are not worn with dresses of these periods then the bodice of the dress itself should be mounted on a boned foundation as were the bodices of the middle of the seventeenth century; the boning, of course, should follow that used in the contemporary corset.

The Construction

The following description of stays gives the principles on which they were made during the sixteenth, seventeenth, and eighteenth centuries:

"The Academy of Armoury" by Randle Holme, 1680
Terms used by Taylors

In a WOMANS GOWN there are these several parts, as

The STAYES, which is the body of the Gown before the sleeves are put too, or covered with the outward stuff: which have these peeces in it, and terms used about it.

The FORE PART, or FORE BODY: which is the Breast part, which hath two peeces in it: as,

The RIGHT SIDE of the Fore-body.

The LEFT SIDE of the Fore-body.

The two SIDE PARTS, which are peeces under both Arms on the sides.

The BACK.

The SHOULDER HEADS, or SHOULDER STRAPS; are two peeces that come over the Shoulders and are fastned to the Fore-body: through which the Arms are put.

SCOREING, or STRIK LINES on the Canvice to sow straight.

STITCHING, is sowing all along the lines with close stitches to keep the Whale-bone each peece from other . . . is the cleaving of the Whale-Bone to what substance or thickness the workman pleaseth.

BONING THE STAYS, is to put the slit Bone into every one of the places made for it between each stitched line which makes Stayes or Bodies stiff and strong.

CORDY ROBE SKIRTS to the Staies are such stayes as are cut into Labells at the bottom, like long slender skirts.

LINING THE BODIES, or STAYES: is covering the inside of the Stayes with Fustian, Linnen, and such like.

BINDING THE NECK, is sowing Galloon at the edge of the Neck.

EYLET HOLES, or EIGLET HOLES, little round holes whip-stitched about, through which laces are drawn to hold one side close to the other.

THE WAIST, is the depth of the Stayes from the Shoulders to the setting on of the skirts: now it is distinguished by the Back Waiste, and the fore body Waist, which is each side of the Stomacher.

SIDE-WAISTED, is long or deep in the Body.

SHORT-WAISTED, is short in the body.

The STOMACHER, is that peece as lieth under the lacings or binding on of the Body of the Gown. Which said body is sometimes in fashion to be:

OPEN BEFORE, that is to be laced on the Breast.

OPEN BEHIND, laced on the Back, which fashion hath always a Maid or Woman to dress the wearer.

The PEAKE, is the bottom or point of the Stomacher, whether before or behind.

A BUSK, it is a strong peece of Wood, or Whalebone, thrust down the middle of the Stomacher to keep it streight and in compass, that the Breast nor Belly shall not swell too much out. These Buskes are usually made in length according to the necessity of the Persons wearing it: if to keep in the fullness of the Breasts, then it extends to the Navel; if to keep the Belly down, then it reacheth to the Honour.

A POINT.

COVERING the Bodies or Stayes, is the laying the outside stuff upon it, which is sowed on the same after diverse fashions: as,

SMOOTH COVERED

108   *c.* 1858. "Jeune dame à la mode, faisant faire un point à sa Jupe." Riveting a crinoline was a favourite subject of the cartoonist when steel cage petticoats first appeared

109   *c.* 1865. "Madame pourra se tenir dans la pièce de devant ... sa crinoline trouvera naturellement sa place dans l'autre." The enormous volume behind achieved by the crinoline in the late sixties was another cartoonist's delight

Both from contemporary prints

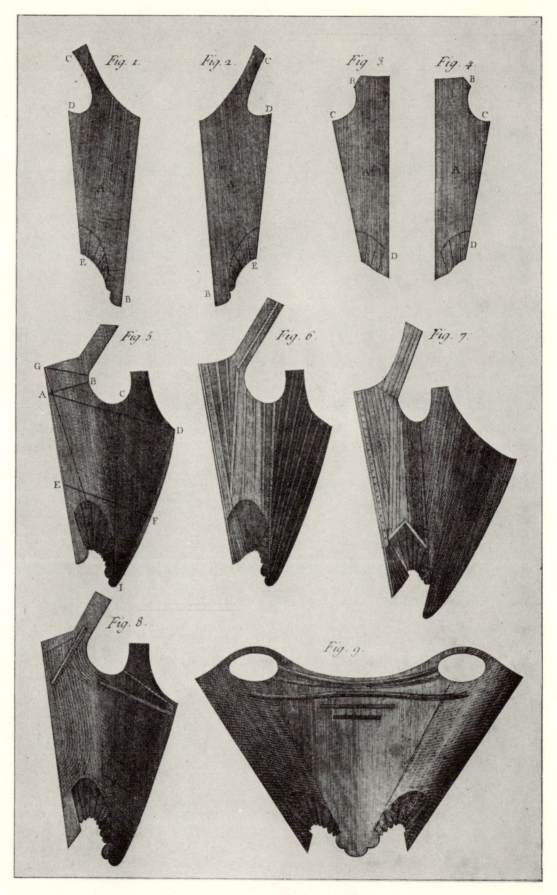

110   **1751.** 1 and 2, Patterns of front of stays; 3 and 4, Patterns of back of stays; 5, Measurements; 6, Half-boned stays; 7, Fully-boned stays; 8 and 9, Inside of stays, showing construction and shaping bones

From Diderot's " L'Encyclopédie"

PLEATED or WRINKLED in the covering.

The WINGS, are WELTS or PEECES set over the place on the top of the Shoulders, where the Body and Sleeves are set together: now Wings are of diverse fashions, some narrow, others broad, some cut in slits, cordy Robe like, others Scalloped.

Eighteenth-century Stays

These directions are based on those given in a pamphlet "Le Tailleur de Corps de Femmes et Enfants", by M. de Garsault, Paris 1769. The diagrams are from Diderot's *Encyclopédie*, Vol. IX, "Le Tailleur d'Habits et Tailleur de Corps", Paris, 1751 (110).

There are two kinds of stays: those which are laced up the back only, and those which are laced up both back and front. The former have the busk inserted up the centre front, while the latter usually have a separate stomacher piece which has the busk up the centre.

A distinction is made between covered stays and stitched stays: stitched stays are in plain cotton, linen, or silk, and all the stitching which separates the whalebone is visible; covered stays have an extra layer of richer material which hides the stitching.

The Measurements

> AB—Centre back to arm-hole.
> CD—Centre front to arm-hole.
> AD—Centre back to centre front.
> EF—Waist.
> CH—Centre back to side waist.
> DI—Length centre front.

Materials

Two layers of material are required, the top one of a closely woven linen or cotton, and the bottom one of a stiff drill or tailor's canvas (formerly "buckram", a coarse linen stiffened with glue or paste).

Construction

Take sufficient drill for the size and style of stays to be made, fold in two and place the paper pattern on it: check pattern with measurements, altering size when necessary, then mark the outline with a tracing wheel. Unfold the drill and draw with a pencil the outlines for both sides of the stays, then cut these out, leaving a quarter of an inch for turning.

Take each piece of the stays and tack it firmly to a corresponding piece of calico; after they have all been mounted in this way, draw with a ruler on each piece of drill lines a quarter of an inch apart, as in the directions given in Fig. 7—this is for fully-boned stays. For half-boned stays the lines are as shown in Fig. 6.

Now all the pieces must be machined very straight along each line; in this way all the spaces between the stitching make cases to hold the whalebones. Up to the eighteenth century whalebone was bought in plates and the staymaker had to cut it himself, but now it can be bought in strips of various lengths about a quarter of an inch wide. There is another variety, sold by the yard, called "feather-bone"; this is made from two narrow strips of bone stitched together with cotton, which can be easily removed if narrower

111. Carved wood busk. Decorated busks of wood, whalebone, or horn were used as late as the early nineteenth century

strips of bone are desirable. Care must always be taken to check the width of the whalebone before ruling the lines which hold it.

Cut the strips of whalebone into the required lengths and round off and file smooth each end: when they are ready push them between the two rows of stitching, beginning with the centre bones of each piece. In the two back pieces a space should be left after each centre back bone for the eyelet holes; turn in the raw edges along the centre backs, and face them with a strip of drill two inches wide; then the eyelet holes should be punched through the three thicknesses of material.

Tack all the boned pieces firmly together and attach the shoulder-straps. Press from the inside with a hot iron, and while the bones are warm curve them into shape—if possible place on a dress stand to cool.

The stays are now ready for fitting, when any adjustments should be marked; shoulder-straps always require attention as shoulders vary very much in height, and the straps should fit very tightly over the shoulder, or top of the arm, to hold the stays in their correct position on the body.

After the fitting, undo the stitches and carefully correct any alterations; the pieces can now be put together again and machined. The seams should be pressed open and the raw edges neatly stitched down flat to the stays. Bind all round the top and shoulder-straps, also round the tabs at the bottom, with a cross-way strip of cotton or bias-binding as sold ready-cut.

The stays are now ready for the extra shaping-bones, which should be firmly sewn inside in the positions shown in Fig. 9; whalebone strips should have been previously curved to shape by heating, or if steels are used they should have been bent to shape. Bones should also be placed in the back from the shoulder-straps across the shoulder-blades to make them as flat as possible. A narrow band of buckram (as sold to-day) should be stitched round the top of the front, and sometimes a piece is also put at the end of the stomacher, centre front. Remember when inserting all these shaping pieces to hold the stays in such a way that the bones, etc., give the requisite roundness and form. Press the stays with a hot iron.

To finish the shaping, a strip of drill should be stitched inside the centre front from top to bottom, wide enough to hold the busk: in sewing pinch in the bottom of the stays to give roundness. The busk should be a heavier piece of whalebone, but as that is now unobtainable a strong steel can be used; it should have a slight curve in where the waist comes.

The stays are now finished except for the covering, that is if they are to be covered with a richer material. This can be cut from the original pattern, slightly larger, or fitted over the stays if different lines of seaming are desired. The pieces are machined together then placed and sewn on to the stays. A lining of a soft cotton material should be stitched inside.

Loops or hooks are often sewn to the tabs at the waist and low down centre front and centre back, to which the petticoats can be attached, otherwise they are inclined to ride up and spoil the line of the corset.

The stays are now ready for wear.

Half-boned stays are much less work than fully-boned ones and give a very good shape.

Shaping-bones were not usual before 1700. If the strip of buckram is placed along the the top of the front and a triangular piece down the centre front, the shaping bones can be omitted; this extra shaping depends, however, on the amount of roundness desired and also on the figure of the woman who is wearing the stays.

Nineteenth- and Twentieth-century Corsets

As corsets of this period are often very small, some of the patterns may need enlarging. Again the back may be too narrow; nineteenth-century corsets are usually too short in the body for a modern woman and may need lengthening.

The exaggerated small waist so fashionable from the middle of the nineteenth century makes these corsets rather uncomfortable and one rarely succeeds in lacing them down to the required size. When first put on no attempt should be made to tight-lace; after an hour's wear it will be found possible to draw the laces much closer. Padding placed inside the corset on bust and hips will help to give the exaggerated curves which otherwise can only be achieved by years of tight-lacing.

The Victorian and Edwardian silhouette changed with every decade but always retained the wasp-waist, and this can only be attained by wearing a corset and being tight-laced. The dresses themselves were always heavily boned, but the strain is too great even when they fasten with lacing. The straight, unboned frocks worn just before and just after the First World War lose a lot of their own particular style if no foundation garments are used.

Early Nineteenth-century Corsets
"The Workwoman's Guide", by a Lady, 1838

Stays or Corsets

It is impossible to give any particular patterns or sizes of stays, as they must, of course, be cut differently according to the figure, and be variously supported with more or less bones or runners of cotton, according to the age, strength, or constitution of the wearer; we shall therefore, confine ourselves to a few observations on the making up: and with respect to the cutting out, it is recommended to those who make their own stays . . . to purchase a pair from an experienced stay-maker that fit perfectly well, and also a pair cut out, but not made up, so as to be a good pattern for the home-made stays.

Woman's Stays

If for ladies, they are made of sattine, or best French jean, which is half a yard wide, and about 20d. or 2s. per yard; if of an inferior quality, they are made of white, brown, grey, or nankeen jean, at 8d. or 10d. per yard, and lined with calico between the doubles. The stay is generally lined between the two pieces of jean with union cloth or Irish linen in every part excepting the gores. Stays are usually cut in four parts, all of which are generally upon the cross, as this assists materially in making them set better to the figure. Two of the pieces reach from each side of the back, nearly to the hips, and the other

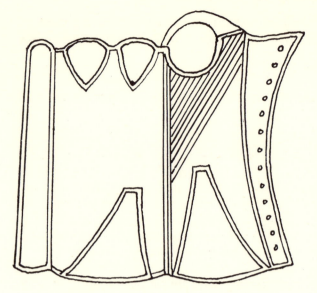

112. Early Nineteenth-century Corset (*1838*)

two from thence to the middle of the busk or steel. There are two gores on each side for the bosom, and two larger ones on each side below, for the hips.

The necessary bones are as follows:

A steel in the middle, which should be narrower at the top than at the bottom, and confined in a strong wash leather, before being put into the stay-case.

Two bones at the extreme ends to prevent the holes from bursting beyond the edge. We may also add, as they are in common use, a second bone down each back, on the other side of the lace holes.

Bones between the front bosom gores, on each side: but these should be very thin and elastic, and are seldom wanted unless the wearer requires much additional support.

Two other bones, one on each side, from about a nail below each arm-hole to the bottom of the stay.

A few slight rib or cross-bones are sometimes put in.

It is as well to observe that unless particularly feeble, or otherwise an invalid, it is most desirable to wear as few bones as possible; and that for healthy persons, the two back bones, with the steel in front, are quite sufficient. The casing of the steel in front is sometimes made of elastic to the depth of four nails from the top, by means of Indian rubber runners; which adds much to the comfort of asthmatic or delicate persons. On each side of the steel is a cotton runner, and these are also put in various other parts of the stays, according to fancy (112).

On Making Up

The needles used for making stays are called the *between needles*. Strong sewing silk, called stay-silk, is used for the best corsets, and strong waxed cotton for the common ones. In sewing the seams, take great care to turn in the work properly, so as to have all the rough edges within the stay; for this purpose, first turn down the outside and inside piece of jean lying on one side of the seam, with the rough edges and the lining prepared as if for common sewing; do the same with the other side of the seam, placing the two seams thus prepared side by side, and sew them firmly together. It will have the effect of a double ordinary seam, when held between finger and thumb. The mode of sewing these four thicknesses so as to make them lie flatly when opened, is rather peculiar. Take up with your needle, three of the thicknesses, leaving the fourth unsewed. The next stitch, take again three folds, leaving the other outside one unsewed: continue alternately taking up one outside and omitting the other, letting the stitches lie close together: when completed, open the seam, and flatten it with the finger and thumb.

The gores are next laid between the doubles of jean, and neatly back-stitched all round; the narrow parts at the top being worked in button-hole stitch.

The bone-cases are then made, and the cotton runners back-stitched.

The oylet or lace-holes are next worked, and after the stay-bones are put in, the top and bottom of the stays, with the shoulder-straps, are neatly bound with stay-binding.

Gores

These are sometimes made of elastic wires, and sometimes of Indian rubber, and sometimes of elastic twill.

Shoulder-Straps

Are made of the same material as the stays, and back-stitched to the front and back of the shoulder.

Sometimes they are buttoned down in the front, which enables the wearer, by unbuttoning them, to dress her hair in an evening with perfect ease, others have oylet-holes to admit of bobbins which lace them to corresponding holes in the stays.

Lace-Holes

Are generally worked in button-hole stitch. Others insert in every hole a ring, called a patent lace-hole; these are very durable, but are said to destroy the laces.

Modesty-Piece

To the top of the stay is sometimes attached a small modesty-piece, which for some people is an excellent contrivance, as it makes it set more closely and delicately in front. The extra piece is all in one, and is the cross-way; it is carried along the whole of the front of the stay; it is about half a nail deep over the bosom, and sloped off to a quarter of a nail over the stay-bone; at the top of this additional strip, which is bound all round, a bobbin is run to draw it up. When drawn properly, this modesty lies over the bosom so as to shade it delicately, whereas, if it were cut all in one piece with the stay it would make it higher, but it would stand out, and not answer the desired end.

N.B. Although this description advises cutting these stays on the cross of the material, existing specimens are usually on the straight. If these early 19th Century stays are cut from four pieces only, the cross-way of the material would certainly give a better fit and a more subtle shape.

Early Twentieth-century Corset

"Up-to-date Dress Cutting and Drafting", Part IV,

by M. Prince Browne   1908

N.B. To make use of the following instructions it would be advisable first to cut a block bodice pattern from a period dress stand which has the desired silhouette.

To Make a Corset Pattern

This should be done from a bodice pattern, cut to seven inches below the waist.

Place a sheet of brown paper on a deal table or board, and, with a piece of tailor's chalk and a rule, draw a line straight across the centre of the paper. Place the two pieces of the front of the bodice pattern with the waist line *on* the chalk line just drawn, and pin them securely in this position to the table or board, with drawing pins.

Place the "Side piece" next the "Side front", with the "Waist line" *on* the chalk line, and pin it down securely in this position. Next place the "Side body", then the "Back", and pin them in the same way.

From the waist line, measure and mark the *height above*, and the *length below* the waist, that the Corset is to be, and draw round each piece of the pattern, round the top and round the bottom to the shape desired—being *very careful* to make each piece correspond in length at the seam, with the one to which it is to be joined.

Take a single tracing wheel, and wheel *close* to the edge of each piece of the bodice pattern as far *above* the waist, and as far *below* the waist, as the outline of the Corset.

Next wheel round the outline for the top and for the bottom of the Corset, and through the waist-line of each piece.

Remove the pattern, and the Corset will be found to be outlined with wheel marks on the sheet of paper.

Draw a chalk line at a distance of half an inch beyond the front line—and another half an inch beyond the back line.

Before cutting out the pattern, number each piece *above* the "Waist line"—the "Fronts" 1–2, the "Side piece" 3, the "Side body" 4, and the "Back" 5.

If this is not done, it will be found very difficult to join the pattern correctly together.

The *top* of each piece will be easily distinguished by having the number above the "*Waistline*".

Now cut piece 1 from the corset pattern, following the *chalk line down the front*, and the wheel marks which outline 2, 3, 4, but *do not cut through the waistline*.

Now cut out part 5, following the *chalk line down the back*, and the wheel marks outlining the top, bottom, and side, *but do not cut through the waistline*.

The corset pattern is now ready for use (113).

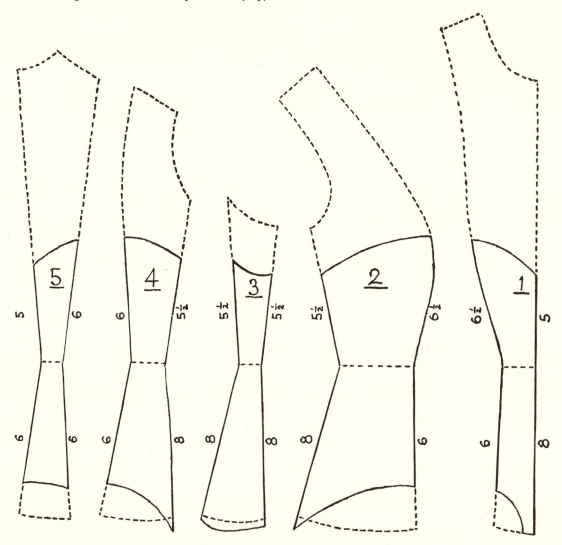

113.   The Corset Pattern

Cutting out the Material, and Lining

Take the material from which the Corsets are to be made, and fold it lengthwise (and wrong side out)—the two selvedges together—and place it on the table.

Take the piece of the pattern marked 1, and place it on the material with the "Front line" *close to*, but not on the selvedge, and with the "Waist line" *perfectly straight* across the material, and pin it down.

Next take the piece of the pattern marked 2, and place it *close* to No. 1, so as to cut the material to the best advantage without waste, being careful that the pattern is placed lengthwise, and the "Waist line" *perfectly straight* across the material, and pin it down.

Now place the pieces marked 3, 4, and 5, all on the material with the "Waist line" *straight across* it, and pin them securely down.

The line of wheel marks down the "Front", and down the back of the pattern—half an inch from the cut edge—must now be traced through on to the material with the wheel, also the "Waist line".

No turnings are allowed, unless the material is one that "frays" easily, in which case extra turnings must be allowed—cut out each piece *very carefully* the *exact* size of the pattern.

Unpin the pattern from each piece of the material, and with a pencil, lightly number it *above* the "Waist line" to correspond with the pattern—of course on the wrong side of the material!

Fold the lining for the Corsets in exactly the same way as the material was folded; place, and pin, the pieces of the pattern on it in the same way, i.e. with the "Waist line" *perfectly straight across*.

With the tracing wheel, mark all the "Waist lines" and the line of wheel marks down the front and back.

No turnings being required, cut out each piece very carefully the *exact* size of the pattern.

Unpin the pattern from the lining, and with a pencil, lightly number *above* the "Waist line", to correspond with the pattern.

To Make the Corsets

Pin, and then tack, the seams of the *lining* of one half of the Corset together, being careful to make the waist line of each piece *exactly meet,* so that when the half Corset is tacked together, the wheel marks may form one unbroken line.

Pin, and tack, the lining of the other half of the Corset in the same way—being careful to make the two halves "face", and not both for the same side.

Machine stitch all the seams carefully, about one-eighth of an inch from the edge.

Measure the two halves together to see that the seams of each half exactly correspond, and that they are *exactly* the same size. Then press the seams open.

Make a turning of one-quarter of an inch down the "Front", and down the "Back", and "notch" the *latter* at the "Waist", to allow the turnings to lie flat: tack and press down these turnings.

The turnings must be made on the same side as the seams.

Leave the top and bottom of the lining "raw edge", for the present.

The lining for the *half* Corset should now measure three-quarters of an inch less than the bodice pattern.

Take piece No. 1 of the material and tack it down the centre of No. 1 of the lining; with the *wrong* side of the material facing the wrong side of the lining, *covering the raw edges of the seams.*

Next take No. 2, tack down the centre of No. 2, of the lining, *with the edge overlapping No. 1*—and the wrong side of the material against the wrong side of the lining covering the raw edges of the seams. In the same way take piece No. 3—then No. 4, then No. 5—*each piece overlapping the edge of the last.* Turn in one-eighth of an inch or more on each seam to face the lining, and tack it neatly and securely down to each seam.

Make a turning of one-quarter of an inch down the front, and tack it to exactly correspond with the turned down edge of the lining, but do not tack the two edges together, as the busks must be inserted between them.

Make a turning of one-quarter of an inch down the back, and "notch" this turning at the waist, to allow it to lie flat and exactly correspond with the turned down edge of the lining, and tack them together closely to the edge. Machine stitch down *each seam, as near as possible to the turned-down edge.*

Do *not* stitch down the back.

Do the other half of the Corset in the same way.

Commence at the "Front", and, from the row of stitching connecting pieces 1 and 2, measure and mark, towards the back, the width of the whalebone, and draw a line to the exact width from the top to bottom of the Corset; tack down this line (the material to the lining).

Take one of the pieces of whalebone and slip it into the space between the row of stitching and the row of tacking, to ascertain whether it is the right width, and then take the bone out again. At the next row of stitching—connecting pieces 2 and 3—measure, mark, and tack down *three* spaces for bones—at the next row of stitching connecting pieces 3 and 4, measure, mark, and tack down *three* spaces for bones.

At the row of stitching connecting pieces 4 and 5 form two more spaces in the same way; then from the row of tacking down the back edge, measure and mark two more spaces—the first of these is for a bone, and the second is for the eyelets—tack and stitch down this *second* space. Cut a strip of stout linen or drill about half an inch wide—on the straight—selvedge-wise—fold it in two *lengthwise*— and press it double. Unpick the tacking from the edge of the back, and insert the strip of linen, or otherwise, between the material and the lining, as *close as possible to the row of stitching just made*, and tack it down firmly—this is to strengthen the Corsets under the eyelets—now tack and stitch down the next mark and complete the space for the eyelets. Again tack down the two edges of the back, close to the edge, and stitch it. This completes the space for the bone at the back, beyond the eyelets.

Machine stitch *all* the spaces for the bones.

It is most important that all these spaces should be made *exactly* the right width to take the bones; neither too narrow nor so wide that the bones will twist—making the Corsets uncomfortable and spoiling the shape.

From the edge of the front of the Corset—measure, and mark, the width of the busk, and draw a line, to the *exact* width from the top to the bottom. Tack down this line, and then machine stitch it.

Do the same with the second half of the Corset.

Take the busk with the eyes on it, and insert it between the lining and the material of the right front, and sew the two edges together by hand.

Take the busk with the studs on it, and insert it between the lining and the material of the left front. Mark the *exact* position in which each stud will be, and pierce a hole for each with a stiletto—pass the studs through the holes and sew the two edges of the Corset together.

Measure and cut off the whalebone to the required length. The bones should only reach to within half an inch or three-quarters of an inch from the raw edges of the Corsets. After the bones have been cut, they must be rounded and scraped at each end (to prevent thickness).

Insert a strip of the bone into each space except the one for the eyelets.

Neatly stitch (by hand) the material to the lining—*close* to, and *round*, the top, and bottom of each bone, to keep them firmly in position.

Steels can be used instead of whalebone under the arms if preferred, but this must of course be decided before forming the spaces.

Measure the width of the steels instead of the whalebone, and be careful to get them the right length, remembering that, like the bones, they must only reach to within one-half or three-quarters of an inch from the raw edge of the Corset.

The Corsets can now either be bound round the top and bottom with Prussian binding, or with satin ribbon (if the Corset is made of satin), and the top can be trimmed with lace, or embroidered.

The bones must be "fanned" with twist at both ends.

Measure and mark the position for the eyelet holes. Be careful to place the marks exactly in the centre of the space, and at the waist place two closer together than the others, as at this point the stay-lace will be drawn through to tie.

A very nice combined "punch" and "eyelet fastener", also the eyelets, can now be purchased. It is the simplest thing in the world to punch the holes and insert the eyelets.

It is an improvement to have three laces instead of one long one—one from the top to the waist, the other for the waist, and the third from the waist to the bottom of the Corsets. This enables the wearer to tighten the Corsets at the waist without affecting the "spring" below the waist, and does not contract the chest.

A small bow stitched to the top of the busk makes a pretty finish, and a small cushion (about two inches square) made of ribbon, stuffed with cotton-wool, and delicately scented, stitched by one corner to the top of the busk on the inside of the Corsets, is an improvement (114).

Sew suspenders to the front of the Corsets, and to the sides also. The Corsets are now finished.

To Simplify

The labour involved in making Victorian and Edwardian corsets can be considerably reduced by using one layer of material only, in which case a heavy drill should be chosen.

Cut out, mark, and tack the corsets together very carefully as in previous directions; after fitting corrections have been made the corsets can be finished as follows:

Always lap seam gussets and basque insertions. Lap seam the long seams—if these are boned the "lap" and two rows of machine stitching should be wide enough to take the whalebone or steel, *or* the latter can be machined and pressed open, the raw edges of these

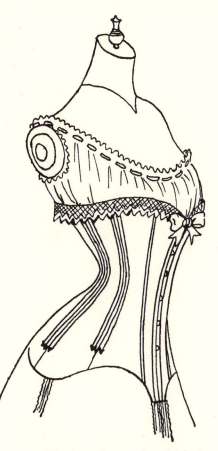

114. The 1908 Corset when finished

seams then neatened by a piece of tape machined down with two rows of stitching, spaced, if necessary, to take whalebone or steel. Tapes should also be machined along the boning lines wherever more bones are required.

It is not always possible to buy front-opening busks; in that case the centre front should be machined together, faced with a strip of drill, and two strong steels inserted, one on either side of the centre front. Strengthen the two centre backs by facing each with a double strip of drill about one inch wide so that the eyelet holes are made through three thicknesses of material.

Bind round top and bottom of the corsets after they have been boned. "Fan" the bones, that is hold them in position by herringbone or other similar stitching.

APPENDIX II

The Construction of Farthingales, Hoop Petticoats, Etc.

No farthingales appear to have survived to show how they were made, but an old Spanish tailor's book, *Libro de Geometria y Traca*, 1589, by J. Alcega, gives the following pattern and instructions:

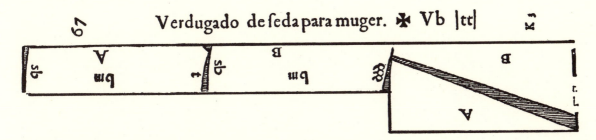

115. "To cut this silk farthingale one half of the material must be folded over the other half making a fold on one side; from the left side the front and then the back of the farthingale are cut out in the doubled silk; the remainder of the silk should be spread out and doubled full width and then the gores cut out with the widest part of one alongside the narrowest part of the other. It should be noted that the front gores go straight to straight and the back gores across to straight, so that on the sides of this skirt there will be no cross and will not drop. The front will have more fullness than the back; with the silk which is left over a valance can be added. The length of the farthingale is a "vara" and a half, and the width round the bottom slightly more than thirteen handspans, which in my opinion is full enough for the farthingale, if more fullness is wanted it can be added to the pattern."

vara—about 2 ft. 8 ins.

In working out a pattern for these boned petticoats it must be remembered that in order to control the shape the bones should lie as far as possible on the weft weave of the material. The exception is the side panels of the eighteenth-century French panier; in this case this particular construction gives a more subtle curve to the skirt—if the straighter English panier is wanted, these panels should be cut on the straight of the material and less gored on the side seams.

Hip-rolls, hip-pads, and the "cushion" bustles should be cut the cross-way of the material; in this way a more rounded line is given when they are filled with cotton-wool, kapok, horsehair, etc.

A single layer of a strong cotton material, such as calico, is suitable for all boned skirts; the facings to take the bones are strips cut on the straight of the material if the lines are straight, cross-way if the lines are curved.

Whalebone is no longer sold in long enough strips, but "crinoline steel" can be bought by the yard; it usually comes in two widths: half an inch and a quarter of an inch.

The early forties' and fifties' crinolines should not have steels; rows of cording or a wide band of horsehair canvas round the bottom of the petticoat should give sufficient stiffening.

Very large crinoline frames are rare; layers of starched petticoats over a small frame are always more successful as they soften the hard lines of the steels, which otherwise look exceedingly ugly when visible through the dress. The same applies to bustles; layers of horsehair canvas flounces, or pleatings, can be arranged on the back of the petticoat— their position and size regulated by the date and style of dress for which the bustle is being made. For the exaggerated eighties' bustle, steels can first be inserted in the back panel of the petticoat before the flounces are added. Contemporary magazines illustrate the infinite variety of ways and materials in which bustles were made.

APPENDIX III

Supports for Corsets, Crinolines, Etc.

ALTHOUGH whalebone was early recognised as the ideal material for stiffening bodices and skirts, so that they soon became, and still are, known as "boned" bodies, "boned" stays, etc., it was often scarce and expensive and various substitutes were used —wood and horn for busks, cane for stays and petticoats. Eventually in the middle of the nineteenth century steel replaced whalebone in crinolines and bustles. At first steel was not flexible enough for the very shaped corsets so, as well as cane, a new support, "Featherbone", made its appearance at the end of the century and became very popular owing to its cheapness. The improvement in the manufacture of steel, however, continued, and during the twentieth century "steels" replaced "bones", though whalebone was also used as late as the 1920's. If modern foundation garments are boned at all it is with very flexible steels and the new "plastic bones"; whalebone is no longer used.

October 1887

We have all heard, almost too much, of the scarcity of whalebone, and the consequent increase in price of the best corsets, and also of "dressmaker's trimmings" as all the etcs. which mount up our bills are termed. If we have suffered in our pockets the poor whale has suffered in person, and like ourselves will rejoice in the American introduction of "Featherbone", a good substitute for whalebones, being unbreakable and unalterable by heat, cold, or weather; "Featherbone" is flexible, and is far better adapted for ordinary dresses than either whalebone, steel, or any other substitute for whalebone.

November 1890

Now that the price of whalebone is so very high, and likely to become higher still, a thoroughly satisfactory substitute for it is a great want of the age; most of these substitutes fail in one respect or another, some are too stiff, others too slight and flexible; one kind will snap in two at slight pressure, another will refuse to bend under any amount; but it seems to me that the happy medium has been found in the new "Platinum" Dress Bones, which are free from the ordinary disadvantages of metal bones. The metal employed for them is an amalgam of silver, steel and platinum, and is extremely flexible and not liable to rust; the bones have, in fact, all the flexibility of whale bone and the strength and firmness of steel, without the tendency to split of the one and to snap of the other.

Myra's Journal

August 1895

A new method of boning dresses recently devised by Mr. G. B. Weekes, of Paris. Featherbone, which is the name of the article employed, is an ingenious commodity resembling whalebone in many respects, but superior to it in others. It is made out of the quills of geese and turkeys by a special process, a large factory having been erected for its manufacture at St. Just, which gives employment to many hundreds of girls and women. The bone, which is light, pliable, and unbreakable, is sold ready cased in boxes of a dozen yards.

The Queen

Manufacture of Crinolines, c. 1858

The largest firm of crinoline manufacturers was that of Thomson's in London, which had branches in New York, Paris, and Brussels, as well as others in Saxony and Bohemia. The London factory alone employed over a thousand women and turned out between three and four thousand crinolines daily. The number of hooks and eyes required amounted to a quarter of a million a day. In twelve years the branch in Saxony alone manufactured 9,597,600 crinolines. The quantities of material required for such an enormous output may be gathered from the fact that the steel wire for the frames of all these skirts amounted to many times the circumference of the earth.

Ciba Review, No. 46, "Crinoline and Bustle"

A firm in Sheffield has taken an order for 40 tons of rolled steel for Crinoline, and a foreign order has been given for one ton a-week for several weeks. *Punch*, July 18, 1857

APPENDIX IV

Whalebone

No study of corsets and crinolines can be complete without some knowledge of whalebone and its history. Whalebone is the name given to the long horny plates or blades, which in one group of whales, the "Right Whales", take the place of teeth. These plates are set in the upper palate at right angles to the long axis of the head and spaced behind each other at a distance of a quarter of an inch. The number of plates on each side ranges from 260 to 360; they are about 10 to 12 inches at the base and from 9 to 13 feet in length. The number, as well as the quality, varies with the species and size of whale. Each plate is triangular in form; its outer edge hard and smooth, the inner edge frayed out into long bristly fibres so that the roof of the whale's mouth inside looks as if it were covered with hair. These fringed blades make a sieve to strain from the sea the small fish or crustacea on which whalebone whales feed.

"Baleen", the more correct name for whalebone, or whale's fins, is a substance in appearance like horn, formed from an agglomeration of hair covered with enamel, and is, in fact, a transition from hair to horn. The hair fibres run parallel and quite even so that a plate of baleen may be split its entire length to any degree of thinness without impairing its peculiar quality of lightness, elasticity, and flexibility. When softened in hot water or by applying heat, it retains any given shape provided it is secured in that shape until cold.

The separation of the whalebone plates from the gums is done at sea; they are then washed in salt water and thoroughly dried before being packed. After delivery at the factory the hair is stripped from the blades, which are soaked in tepid water for two or three weeks and then subjected to steam for about an hour, after which they are ready to be cut into strips of the required size. As whalebone is a natural product the blades vary very much in texture, and considerable skill and experience are required to estimate their quality and prepare them for the needs of the market.

The peculiar qualities of whalebone made it extremely suitable for shaping corsets and boned petticoats; it is not surprising, therefore, to find a very close relationship between the history of the three periods when these boned garments were worn and the three periods of great whale fisheries, and that the vanity of women has contributed not a little to the chase and destruction of this now rare and interesting animal.

The Atlantic Right Whale (Nordcaper or Sarda) was the object of the first regular whale fishery, that of the Basques, which originated probably about a thousand years ago in the Bay of Biscay. The value of whalebone must have been early known, for in 1150 King Sancho of Navarre granted certain privileges to the city of San Sebastian, and in the grant there is a list of articles of merchandise with the duties that must be paid for warehousing them; whalebone has a prominent place in the list.

One can only guess the early uses made of whalebone, but it is occasionally mentioned in connection with mediaeval dress, as, for instance, plumes on helmets, stiffening for the elaborate women's headdresses, and the long peaked shoes. When stiffened bodies and farthingales appeared in the sixteenth century it could not have been long before the superiority of whalebone over wood and cane supports brought it into use wherever available. The first description of the Biscay whale was given by Ambroise Paré, who visited Biarritz in 1564; he described how "des lames qui sortent de la bouche, on en fait des vertugals, busques pour les femmes". Although records are scarce a considerable trade in whalebone must have arisen to meet the demand made by the extravagant Elizabethan and Jacobean fashions. In the archives of the City of London there is a letter, dated December 12th, 1607, from the Lord Mayor to the Lords of the Council, enclosing a petition for certain merchants trading to "Biskey", and "such as used the trade of making Vardingales, Boddyes, and Sleeves for Women in and about the City", requesting that the duty proposed, 6d. in the pound upon whalebone-fins, might not be enforced.

The Biscayan whale was hunted to the verge of extinction during the sixteenth century, and the fishery finally declined at the beginning of the seventeenth century, just about the time the farthingale and its accompanying rigid bodice ceased to be worn.

The second great whale fishery was the hunt of the Greenland whale, which was found round Spitzbergen when the voyages for the discovery of the north-east route to the Far East were undertaken at the close of the sixteenth century. Although the English had been pioneers of this fishery the Dutch began whaling there in 1612, and with such success that they soon gained and kept control of the Greenland Fishery until its decline towards the end of the eighteenth century. The Greenland whale was especially valuable for whalebone, the plates attaining a length of from 10 to 15 feet, of superior quality baleen.

Many attempts were made to revive the English Greenland Fishery. In 1672 an Act of Parliament allowed British whalers to land their products free; colonials were admitted at a reduced rate, while foreigners had to pay a customs duty of £9 per ton for oil, and £18 per ton for whalebone. At the beginning of the eighteenth century there was a considerable rise in the price of whalebone, probably caused by the introduction of the hoop petticoat. A 1720 broadsheet describes how whalebone was smuggled into the country to avoid customs duty. An enquiry into the Greenland trade in 1722 states: "As to the Whale-Fins, it appears by the Custom-House Books, that there hath been imported in the Port of London, from the Year 1715, to 1721, one Year with another, about 150 tons yearly, even when the Price hath been very dear, viz. 400 l. per Ton, little more or less, which is, one Year with another, 60,000 l. a Year, over and above what is imported in all other Ports of Great Britain and Ireland; which may moderately be supposed to be 100 Tons more. Then the Sum paid for Whalebone amounts to 100,000 l. per Annum, besides what probably may be run clandestinely: All which hath hitherto been clear loss to the Nation and clear Gain to our Neighbours." Bounties were offered to British whalers and customs duties removed, but English whaling met with no success. Another report in 1771 says: "If the British fishery is given up we must depend almost entirely upon the Dutch who may charge what prices they please (and in fact they have charged as high as

£700 a ton for whale fins) which must make a prodigious annual drain of money from the country."

At the end of the eighteenth century the Greenland Whale Fishery was declining, prices fell—hoop petticoats and whalebone stays were no longer fashionable wear.

The third great whale fishery was the American Fishery of the nineteenth century. Although whales had been hunted off the American coast from the seventeenth century, it was the chase of the great Bowhead whale in the Arctic Ocean which began in the 1840's that established the American Whale Fishery. In the first decades of the nineteenth century the demand for whalebone fell so low that few vessels brought any home; after that, with the return of the corset, prices and demand rose steadily, and when finally, in 1859, petroleum was discovered and took the place of whale-oil, the American Fishery depended almost exclusively on whalebone. The output of whalebone for the whole of the nineteenth century exceeded £90,000,000 worth, about 450,000,000 American dollars.

The peak years of the American Fishery were the middle of the century; from 1860 onwards output of whalebone began to decline. Improved methods of processing steel inspired the first "cage" crinoline in 1856, and thereafter practically all crinolines and bustles were made of flexible steels; the highest grade corsets, however, were still made of whalebone, and the great development of the corset industry at the end of the century continued to levy a heavy toll on the unfortunate whale. In the first decade of the twentieth century the increasing rarity of the Bowhead whale caused prices to soar to fantastic heights; one year as much as £2,800 per ton being paid for it. But the corset was slowly losing the subtle curves that only whalebone could give and, as excellent substitutes were adequate support for the new line, gradually less and less whalebone was used in fashionable corsetry. And once more these changes came just in time to save yet another species of whale from almost complete extinction.

References

Elking, Henry (1722). *A View of the Greenland Trade and Whale Fishery.*

Jenkins, J. T. (1921). *A History of the Whale Fisheries.*

MacPherson, David (1805). *Annals of Commerce.*

Markham, M. C. R. *On the Whale Fishery of the Basque Provinces of Spain.*

Paré, Ambroise (1573). *Des Monstres Marins.*

"Remembrancia preserved among the Archives of the City of London, 1579–1664", 1878.

Stevenson, Charles H. (1907). *Whalebone—Its Production and Utilisation*, U.S.A. Bureau of Fisheries.

GLOSSARY

Aune. Old French measure, about 1·18 metres.

Baleine. Whalebone.

BASQUE. Strip of material shaped to fit the top of the hips.

BASQUINE, VASQUINE (sixteenth century). Close-fitting bodice with tabs or a basque, but in England the word has been used for a petticoat.

BIAS-BINDING. Narrow strip of material cut on the bias, or cross-weave, of material.

BODY (sixteenth century). Close-fitting upper part of woman's dress, either belonging to the gown, or worn as a separate underbodice. *See* PAIR OF BODIES, WHALE-BONED BODY.

BRASSIÈRE, "BRA" (twentieth century). *See* BUST BODICE.

Brassière (seventeenth, eighteenth century). In France a short bodice for négligé wear, now only used for a young child's bodice.

BUMBAST, BOMBAST (sixteenth, seventeenth century). Padding in clothes.

BUSC, BUSK, BUSKE. Long piece of wood, whalebone, horn, steel, etc., placed in the centre front of corset to keep the body erect. Now used for the two strips of steel, one with eyes, the other with studs, which fasten a corset centre front.

Busc, busq, busque. Busk.

BUSK POINT. The lace which tied the busk in position. *See* POINT.

BUST BODICE. Short tight-fitting bodice worn round the bust.

BUSTLE. Artificial structure worn to extend skirts behind.

Cache-corset. Petticoat bodice, camisole.

CAMISOLE. Loose bodice worn over the corset; the earlier name was "petticoat bodice."

CANE. Hollow stem of giant reeds, or solid stem of slender palms, used as a substitute for whalebone in corsets and petticoats. Extremely fine round or flat strips of cane are found in corsets until the end of the nineteenth century.

CASE, CASING. Strip of material stitched to another along both edges to make a slot to contain bones, etc.

Considérations (late seventeenth, late eighteenth century). Hip-pads or rolls.

CORD, CORDING. Strands of twisted or woven threads stitched between two layers of material for stiffening, used in corsets, petticoats, etc.

Corps (sixteenth, seventeenth, eighteenth century). Body, whaleboned body, stays.

CORSET. Close-fitting bodice, stiffened with whalebone, etc. The word was occasionally used in the seventeenth and eighteenth centuries and became fashionable in the nineteenth century.

Corset. From the beginning of the nineteenth century in France this term completely replaces the old word "*corps*".

Criarde (late seventeenth, early eighteenth century). Petticoat stiffened by paste or gum.

CRINOLINE (nineteenth century). Petticoat artificially stiffened by horsehair, whalebone, steel, etc.

Cul postiche (late eighteenth century). False bums, rumps.

Épaulette. Shoulder-strap.

EYELET PUNCH. Instrument which secures the eyelets in position.

EYELETS. Holes made either side of corset-opening through which the lace is threaded. They were originally stitched round, and from the nineteenth century the word is used for the metal rings which replaced the stitching.

FALSE BUMS, RUMPS (late eighteenth century). Pads of wool, horsehair, cork, etc., worn on the hips and behind; also used for farthingales.

FARTHINGALE, VARDINGALL, VERDINGALE (sixteenth, early seventeenth century). Petticoat extended by whalebone, cane, etc., or hip-pads or rolls.

FEATHERBONE. Substitute for whalebone made from goose quills

Garde-infante. Late seventeenth-century Spanish farthingale.

GARTER. Band worn round the knee to keep stockings up.

GUSSET, GORE. Triangular piece of material inserted in a garment to give extra width.

Hausse-cul (sixteenth, early seventeenth century). Padded hip-roll, kind of farthingale.

HIP-PADS, ROLLS. Padded roll worn round the hips; a pair of crescent-shaped pads, one worn on each hip.

HOOPS, HOOP PETTICOAT. Any petticoat extended by whalebone, cane, etc., such as farthingale, crinoline, but more especially the eighteenth-century whaleboned petticoat.

IMPROVER (eighteenth century). Hoop petticoat.

JUMP (eighteenth century). Under bodice similar in shape to stays but looser and without bones.

LACE. Twisted or woven cord of linen, silk, etc., threaded through eyelet holes to draw the two sides of a corset, etc., together.

Lacet. Lace.

LAPSEAM. One edge of seam is lapped or laid over the other with the edges facing in opposite directions and parallel; both edges are stitched.

METAL "MANNEQUIN" MOULD. Dress stand, or "mannequin", of metal. Corsets when finished were starched and fitted on to these moulds and heated from inside to dry out "moulded" to the mannequin's shape.

MODESTY, MODESTY-PIECE. An extra strip of material attached to the top of a corset.

NAIL. An old measure of 2¼ inches.

Œillet. Eyelet.

PAIR OF BODIES, BODYS, BODYES, BODDICE (sixteenth, seventeenth century). Under bodice with stiffening; early corset.

Panier (eighteenth century). Hoop petticoat; when used in the plural it applies to side hoops.

PASTE. Sticky substance, usually made from flour and water, used to stiffen material for corsets, petticoats.

PLACARD. Another word for stomacher.

POCKET HOOPS. *See* SIDE HOOPS.

POINT (Med.–seventeenth century). Tagged lace for lacing bodice, stays, etc., later called "lace".

QUILT, QUILTING. Two layers of material (with or without extra padding between) firmly held together by rows of, or a pattern of, stitching; used to stiffen corsets and petticoats.

Robe battante (eighteenth century). Sack.

SACK, SACQUE (eighteenth century). Dress with pleats behind which hung loosely from the shoulders.

SHAPING-BONES (eighteenth century). Extra strips of whale-bone, etc., placed inside stays to give shape.

SIDE HOOPS, POCKET HOOPS. The hoop petticoat divided in two and as small hoops worn on each hip.

Soutien-gorge. Bust bodice.

STAYS. Term used for seventeenth- and eighteenth-century corsets, still very common in the nineteenth and twentieth centuries.

STOMACHER (sixteenth, seventeenth, eighteenth century). Triangular piece of material placed over, or behind, the front lacing of stays.

Strapontin. 1885 bustle.

SUSPENDER BELT. Waist band to hold suspenders.

SUSPENDERS. Pair of attachments to which stockings are fastened, usually sewn to corsets.

TABS. Tongue-shaped pieces of material obtained by slitting round the edge of a garment to give extra width; or separate pieces of similar shape attached to form a basque.

TAG, TAGGE. Piece of metal wrapped round the end of a lace to keep it from fraying, and to facilitate threading through eyelets.

Tournure (nineteenth century). Bustle.

TRUSS. To tighten upwards, e.g. shoulder-straps to corset.

Vara. An old Spanish measure, about 2 feet 8 inches.

Vertugade, vertugadin, vertugalle. Farthingale.

WAISTCOAT (sixteenth century). Close-fitting body undergarment stopping at the waist.

WHALEBONED BODY (sixteenth, seventeenth century). Term used for early corsets.

GLOSSARY OF MATERIALS USED FOR CORSETS AND PETTICOATS

BATISTE. Fine cotton fabric similar to cambric.

BROCADE. Silk fabric with raised pattern, perhaps with gold or silver threads.

BROCHÉ. Silk or cotton fabric with a satin pattern on the surface.

BUCKRAM. Coarse linen or cloth stiffened with paste or gum.

CAMBRIC. Very fine white linen.

CAMELOT. Brocade (sixteenth, seventeenth century).

CAOUTCHOUC. Indiarubber.

COUTIL. Twilled cotton fabric.

CRINOLINE-ZEPHYR, CRINOLINE-MOUSSELINE. Springy material, being a mixture of fine cotton, or woollen threads, and horsehair.

DAMASK. Silk or linen fabric with pattern which is reversed on the back.

DIMITY. Cotton fabric with stripes or pattern.

DRILL. Twilled linen or cotton fabric.

ELASTIC, ELASTIC WEAVES. Fine threads of rubber, wrapped round with silk or cotton threads to facilitate weaving.

GROS DE NAPLES. Very heavy corded silk, made in Italy.

GROS DE TOURS. The same, made in France.

HORSEHAIR. Unwoven, used for padding; may be woven with cotton or woollen threads. *See* CRINOLINE.

JEAN. Twilled cotton cloth, very strong and heavy.

KERSEY. Light-weight narrow woollen cloth (sixteenth century).

MUSLIN. Very fine transparent cotton material.

NAINSOOK. Muslin.

PERCALE. Fine white calico cloth.

POUX-DE-SOIE. Heavy corded silk.

SATEEN. Cotton or woollen fabric with glossy surface.

SATIN. Silk fabric with glossy surface.

SURAH. Soft twilled Indian silk.

TABBY. Heavy silk, corded and watered (Fr. *Moiré antique*).

TAFFETA. Light, thin, glossy silk fabric.

UNION CLOTH. Stout material, a mixture of linen and cotton much dressed and stiffened.

INDEX

The numerals in **heavy type** refer to the *figure numbers* of the illustrations